The MAILBOX®

The Education Center®

grades ?-K

Day-by-Day ALPHA PLANS

A Week's Worth of Ideas for **Every** Alphabet Letter

- Learning centers
- Group-time activities
- Literature-related ideas
- Gross-motor practice
- Snack ideas
- Management tips

- Art activities
- Songs and rhymes
- Class book ideas
- Patterns and practice pages

"T-rrific"!

Managing Editor: Kimberly Ann Brugger

Editorial Team: Becky S. Andrews, Margaret Aumen, Diane Badden, Tricia Kylene Brown, Kimberley Bruck, Karen A. Brudnak, Karin Bulkow, Amy Erickson Corkhill, Pam Crane, Chris Curry, Roxanne LaBell Dearman, David Drews, Ada Goren, Tazmen Fisher Hansen, Marsha Heim, Lori Z. Henry, Mark Rainey, Greg D. Rieves, Mary Robles, Hope Rodgers-Medina, Rebecca Saunders, Donna K. Teal, Sharon M. Tresino, Zane Williard

www.themailbox.com

©2013 The Mailbox® Books
All rights reserved.
ISBN 978-1-61276-256-2

Printed in the United States
10 9 8 7 6 5 4 3 2 1

HPS246102

Table of Contents

www.themailbox.com/core

The kindergarten skills in this book align to **Common Core State Standards**.
www.themailbox.com/core

What's Inside

Each letter includes

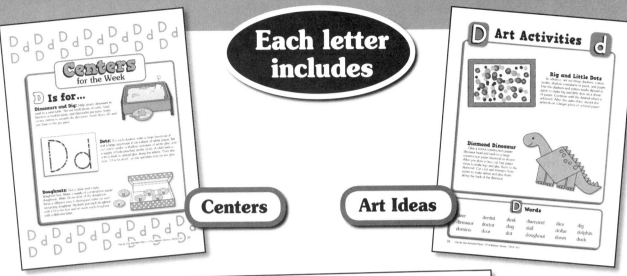

Centers

Art Ideas

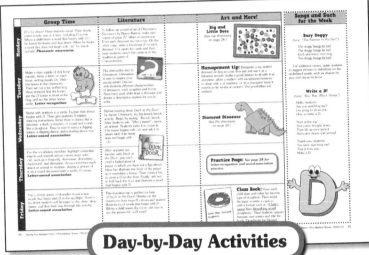

Day-by-Day Activities

Patterns and an Activity Page

online extras!

FREE Online Extras! Go to www.themailbox.com

Alphabet Games

Review a few letters or the entire alphabet with these fun-to-play group games!

Name That Letter!

Invite one child to be a letter detective and stand at the front of the room. Secretly show the rest of the group a letter card. Classmates give letter-related clues—such as words that begin with the letter, tips about forming the letter, and letter sightings in the classroom—until the detective correctly names the mystery letter.

Switch!

Prepare a supply of matching uppercase and lowercase letter cards so there is one card per child. Seat students in a circle and hand out the cards. To play a round, name a letter and then lead students in singing the song. As the group sings, the two students who have the named letter switch places before the end of the song. For added fun, every few rounds say, "Alphabet soup!" instead of a letter. Then, as you sing the song—changing the first, second, and fourth lines to "If you have a letter card"—all students switch places!

(sung to the tune of "The Farmer in the Dell")

If you have the letter [*F*],
If you have the letter [*F*],
Change your places; you must be quick
If you have the letter [*F*].

Letter Delivery

Put a different letter card in each of several envelopes; then put the envelopes in a tote bag. Seat students in a circle and play music. Hand the bag to a volunteer and ask her to walk around the circle pretending to be a mail carrier. When the music stops, the mail carrier delivers an envelope to a nearby classmate. This child removes the card from the envelope and shows the letter to the group. When the group identifies the letter, the student and the mail carrier trade places.

Soup and Crackers

Display a large laminated soup bowl; then use a wipe-off marker to write letters in the soup. Provide sticky notes (crackers). Name a letter and have a volunteer cover a matching letter with a cracker. Or invite a volunteer to name a letter and then cover it with a cracker.

Centers for the Week

A Is for...

Alligator: Attach a cutout copy of the alligator pattern on page 9 to the side of a shoebox. Cut an opening in the mouth. Set out letter tiles or cards that include several As. A child "feeds" the alligator each tile or card with the letter A and sets the other letter manipulatives aside.

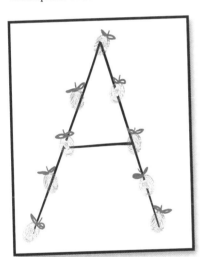

Apple: For each center visitor, provide a sheet of paper on which you have written a large A. Also set out a red ink pad or a shallow container of red paint. A child makes red fingerprints (apples) on the letter. After the prints dry, he draws a stem and leaves on each. For a variation, set out a poster-size piece of paper with a large A and have students put plastic apples side by side on the letter.

Acorn: Write "Aa" on a large construction paper acorn. Set out a sheet of paper on which you have drawn a sad face and letter manipulatives that include several uppercase and lowercase As. Center visitors put each A on the acorn and the other letters on the paper.

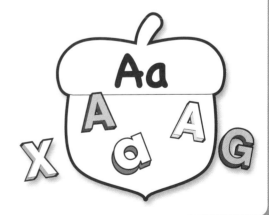

Group Time	Literature
Monday Write As and a few other letters on a sheet of chart paper and then display it within student reach. Invite students to find each *a* and draw an apple around it. ***Letter recognition***	Secretly hide a toy alligator under a table. After you share *There's an Alligator Under My Bed* by Mercer Mayer, discover the alligator with mock surprise. Then have students line up from the table to the door. Invite them to chant "*A* is for *alligator*" as they pass the alligator down the line and out the door!
Tuesday Draw a large simple alligator head. Make a supply of white paper triangles (teeth). Write "A" or "a" on most of the teeth and a different letter on each remaining tooth. Students put each tooth with the letter A in the alligator's mouth and set the other teeth aside. ***Letter recognition***	During a second reading of *There's an Alligator Under My Bed*, have students point out the alligator each time they spot it in an illustration. Invite your young alligator finders to mark each alligator with a sticky note labeled "A."
Wednesday Draw an ant and an ant hill on separate blank cards. Set the cards apart on the ledge of the board or on the floor in your group area. Gather a class supply of letter cards with mostly As. Youngsters sort out the A cards and use them to make a trail between the ant and the ant hill. ***Letter recognition***	Give each child an apple cutout. Instruct him to write "Aa" on it and then attach it to a craft stick. Explain that *apple* begins with A. As you read aloud *The Apple Pie Tree* by Zoe Hall, have each student wave his cutout each time he hears the word *apple*.
Thursday Put on an apron with pockets. Place in the pockets items or pictures that begin with A. Sing "Pick a Pocket!" on page 7 with students several times, each time removing a different item or picture from a pocket and incorporating it into the song. ***Letter-sound associations***	After students are familiar with *The Apple Pie Tree*, set out a poster-size tree cutout with a leafy top. Have students use red paint and A-shaped sponge cutouts to make letter prints all over the treetop. After the paint dries, the tree is a letter-perfect display!
Friday Lead students in the call-and-response chant "Make an A" on page 7 as they write uppercase and lowercase As on their own papers. For a variation, have youngsters write the letters with colorful crayons. ***Writing***	To follow up *The Apple Pie Tree,* have students brainstorm various apple snacks. Then serve each youngster apple slices and fruit dip. As youngsters enjoy their treat, encourage them to name A words.

Pretty Prints

(See the directions on page 8.)

Transition: Divide the class into two groups: alligators and apes. When it's time to transition to a different activity, call students by the corresponding group name. As each student moves, have him quietly imitate his assigned animal.

Amazing Astronaut

(See the directions on page 8.)

Practice Page: *See page 10 for letter-recognition practice.*

Class Book: For the first page, write "The letter ants go marching one by one. They find *A* words just for fun." Then have each child make a fingerprint ant on a sheet of paper and draw something that begins with *A*. Write captions. Then bind the pages.

Sarah's ant sees an apple.

Pick a Pocket!

(tune: "The Farmer in the Dell")

[Apricot] starts with *A*,
[Apricot] starts with *A*.
Hip hip hip hooray!
[Apricot] starts with *A*.

Make an A

For a fun call-and-response chant, say the lines one at a time and have students repeat them.

Make a tent.
Cross it with a line.
That's uppercase *A*;
It's so fine.

Make a ball.
Add a wall.
That's lowercase *a*;
It's so small!

Disappearing Lunch

An ape took my apple.
An alligator drank my punch.
An ant ate my apricot.
Now I don't have a lunch!

Art Activities

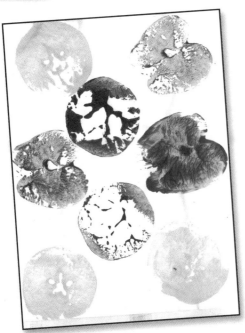

Pretty Prints

In advance, cut one apple in half lengthwise and one apple in half crosswise. Set out paper towels and shallow containers of red, yellow, and green paint. To begin, dip an apple half in paint, pat it on a paper towel to remove the excess paint, and then make a print on a white sheet of paper. Make additional prints until a desired effect is achieved.

Amazing Astronaut

Draw colorful stripes on the legs of a large uppercase *A* cutout. Glue the cutout to a sheet of black paper titled "Astronaut." Illustrate a white circle cutout to make a self-likeness and then glue it to a larger circle cutout (astronaut helmet). Glue the helmet to the triangular opening in the *A*. Glue narrow streamers to the bottom of the letter and then use a white crayon to draw stars on the black paper.

 Words

afraid	alien	alligator	anchor	animals
ant	antelope	antlers	ape	apple
applesauce	apricot	apron	astronaut	ax

Name _____

I Can Find A!

 Circle.

A

A	a	t	A
a	T	g	a
R	A	r	G
A	a	t	a

Day-by-Day Alphabet Plans • ©The Mailbox® Books • TEC61391

Centers for the Week

B Is for...

Boxes: Collect several different-size boxes. Then pair each large box with a small box that fits inside it. After you write an uppercase *B* on each large box and a lowercase *b* on each small box, scramble the boxes. A child names the letters as he nests each small box in a large box. If time allows, he builds with the boxes too!

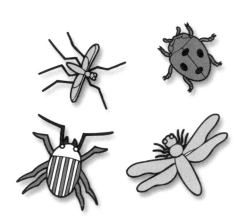

Bugs: Provide paper, a variety of plastic bugs, and a shallow container of paint. Each center visitor uses the bugs to make paint prints on a sheet of paper. For a letter-perfect painting, she makes prints to form the letter *B*.

Basket: Cut out a copy of the picture cards from page 15. Put the cards in a manila envelope and set out a basket labeled with the letter *B*. A child dumps out the cards. Then he names each picture, in turn. If the picture name begins with /b/, he puts the card in the basket. If it does not begin with /b/, he returns it to the envelope. A tisket, a tasket, *B* words in the basket!

Group Time	Literature
Monday — Put letter manipulatives, including several Bs, in a shallow container. Place tongs and an upside-down plastic bowl (hive) nearby. Invite students to take turns as the "B-keeper" by using tongs to remove Bs from the container and then slipping the Bs under the bowl to put them in the hive. **Letter recognition**	Read aloud *Bear Snores On* by Karma Wilson. Then ask students to imagine they are sleeping just as Bear does. Name words, one at a time, including several words that begin with /b/. Whenever students hear a word that begins with /b/, they wake from their slumber and stretch and yawn!
Tuesday — Write letters all over the board, writing mostly Bs and leaving space between the letters. Then ask children to take turns "blowing" bubbles by drawing a circle (bubble) around each B. As you erase the remaining letters, encourage students to imagine that the wind is blowing them away! **Letter recognition**	After students are familiar with *Bear Snores On*, have one student (Bear) "nap" facing away from the class. Give one child a B letter card and each remaining student a different letter card. Youngsters say, "Wake up, Bear!" Then Bear "wakes up" and guesses who has the B. The student with the B is Bear for the next round.
Wednesday — Write Bs and other letters on a beach ball. Stand with students. Then toss the ball to a child. If the letter closest to his right thumb is a b, he says "B is for *bounce!*" Then he bounces the ball to you. If the letter is not B, he rolls the ball to you. Continue until each child has a turn. **Letter identification**	Gather letter cards, including several that show b. Read aloud *Barnyard Banter* by Denise Fleming. Then show youngsters each letter card, in turn. If the card shows a B, each student chants, "B is in the barnyard, /b/, /b/, /b/." If the card does not show B, each student makes a farm animal sound.
Thursday — Title a sheet of chart paper "Bb" and draw a large barn on it. Display it within student reach. Then play lively music. Have each student, in turn, quickly come up and write either B or b on the barn. Encourage students to fill the barn with Bs before the song ends! **Writing letters** 	To follow up *Barnyard Banter*, have students use markers, letter stampers, and letter cutouts to decorate a length of green paper (pasture) with uppercase and lowercase Bs. Showcase the pasture with a blue paper sky and a barn cutout. Then title the display "Bs Are in the Barnyard!"
Friday — Seat students in a circle and hand one child a ball. Youngsters pass the ball around the circle as you play music. When the music stops, the student with the ball names a word that begins with /b/. When the music resumes, the youngsters continue passing the ball. **Letter-sound association**	Illustrate a large B cutout with a face and then present it to students as a book buddy. Set out the two books for the week. Then invite each student to take a turn holding the book buddy and making a comment about the books, such as how they are alike or which book he likes better and why.

Art and More!

"Hand-some" Butterfly
(See the directions on page 14.)

Management Tip: Attach a large *B* sticker to a small Mylar balloon on a stick. Give it to the line leader to hold, use it as a temporary reward for good behavior, or use it to point to a student you wish to call on.

Bell and Ball Painting
(See the directions on page 14.)

Practice Page: *See page 16 for letter-recognition and sound-association practice.*

Class Book: To create the first page, write on a large sheet of paper "The ball bounces..." and attach a sticky dot (ball). To create the remaining pages, give each child a sheet of paper and have him draw something that begins with /b/. Write a corresponding phrase as shown. Then have the child place a sticky dot (ball) on his page to match the caption. Stack the pages and bind them between two covers.

over the book

Songs and Such for the Week

Beautiful *B*
(Tune: "For He's a Jolly Good Fellow")

Invite students to "write" *B*s in the air as they sing this song!

This is a beautiful B.
This is a beautiful B.
This is a beautiful B.
You make it just like this.
You make it just like this.
You make it just like this.
This is a beautiful B.
You make it just like this!

Buzz for *B*!
(Tune: "London Bridge")

Busy Bee says, "Buzz, buzz, buzz!"
"Buzz, buzz, buzz, buzz, buzz, buzz!"
Busy Bee says, "Buzz, buzz, buzz!"
"I start with *B*!"

B Art Activities b

"Hand-some" Butterfly

With adult assistance, make overlapping hand tracings as shown. Use a black crayon to outline a body where your thumbs overlap and then draw a face and two antennae. Write an uppercase *B* on one wing and a lowercase *b* on the other wing. Then color the fancy flier!

Bell and Ball Painting

In advance, gather large jingle bells and a couple small balls. To begin, place a sheet of paper in a lidded container. Put several drops of paint on the paper and then drop the bells and balls into the container and secure the lid. Gently move the container back and forth so the bells and balls roll through the paint and make prints. After a desired effect is achieved, remove the bells and balls. Then take out the paper and allow the paint to dry.

B Words

bag	ball	balloon	band	banjo	barn
basket	bear	bed	bee	bell	birthday
book	bounce	box	bubble	butterfly	buzz

TEC61391

TEC61391

TEC61391

TEC61391

TEC61391

TEC61391

TEC61391

TEC61391

TEC61391

TEC61391

TEC61391

TEC61391

I Know About *B*!

 Color the pictures that begin like .

Circle each **Bb**.

B	r	b	S
R	B	b	m
b	M	B	b

Centers for the Week

C Is for...

Cup: Label a supply of upside-down disposable cups with uppercase and lowercase Cs, writing one letter per cup. Students sort the cups and arrange each set on a work surface to form two large Cs. Then they stack the cups to make pyramids.

Car: Attach a large piece of paper to a table. Draw an uppercase C and a lowercase c bubble-style. Then draw a dashed line on each letter to represent a road. Draw an arrow on each road to direct students to "drive" from the top of each letter to the bottom. Set out toy cars and invite students to "drive" on the C roads as they say, "C is for car."

Cake: Get a construction paper cake and a supply of narrow paper rectangles (candles). Write an uppercase C or a lowercase c on most of the candles and a different letter on each remaining candle. A student puts each candle with C or c on the cake and sets the other candles aside.

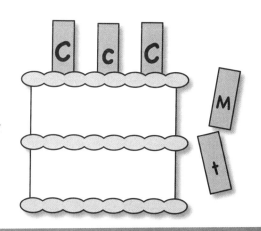

	Group Time	Literature
Monday	Gather a stop sign cutout, a green circle cutout, and a toy car. As you hold up the circle, students "drive" the car by passing it from one student to the next. When you hold up the stop sign, the student with the car pauses and says which of two words you name begins with /c/. **Phonemic awareness**	The day before reading *Caps for Sale: A Tale of a Peddler, Some Monkeys, and Their Monkey Business* by Esphyr Slobodkina, tell students that *caps* starts with C. Encourage each youngster to bring in a cap to wear for storytime. It's sure to add to the reading fun as students imagine the monkeys taking their caps!
Tuesday	Make a supply of candle and flame cutouts. Write a letter on each flame, writing mostly Cs. Display the candles on a cake illustration and put a flame letter-side down on each. Each student, in turn, flips a flame. If the flame shows the letter C, he puts out the candle by taking the flame. **Letter recognition**	After reading aloud *Caps for Sale*, have students pass a cap around as they say, "Caps for sale. Caps for sale. Fifty cents a cap." Each time they complete the chant, the student who has the cap names an object that begins with C. Then youngsters continue, inserting the named object in place of *caps*.
Wednesday	Gather a construction paper cave cutout and a black paper cave opening. Staple the top of the cave opening to the cave. Gather letter cards, including several Cs. Students lift the cave opening and put the cards with C inside. They set the remaining cards aside. **Letter recognition**	Read aloud *The Very Hungry Caterpillar* by Eric Carle. Then hold a leaf cutout and a hole puncher. As students recap the story, hole-punch the leaf each time a student names a story detail. For a variation, punch holes to form the letter C and then display the leaf with student illustrations of caterpillars.
Thursday	Display a cookie jar cutout. Students pass around a container of cookie cutouts as they chant, "*C* is for cookies in the cookie jar." At the end of the chant, the student holding the bag removes a cookie, names a word that begins with /k/, and attaches the cookie to the jar. Youngsters repeat the chant to continue. **Letter-sound association**	To follow up *The Very Hungry Caterpillar*, make a pom-pom caterpillar. Give each student a copy of a picture card from page 21. Have students pass the caterpillar around. Before a child passes the caterpillar, she names her picture and says, "Yum!" if it begins with C and "Not hungry!" if it does not.
Friday	Ask students to imagine they each have a camera that only takes pictures of things that begin with C. Then name words one at a time. When you say a word that begins with /k/, each child says, "Click!" and pantomimes taking a photograph. **Letter-sound association**	For a display related to *The Very Hungry Caterpillar*, give each youngster a paper strip. Have him draw a caterpillar head at the left end. Then instruct him to draw a row of Cs close together to form the caterpillar's body. Showcase students' work with the title "*C* Is for *Cute Caterpillars*!"

Art and More!

Cut, Cut, Cut!
(See the directions on page 20.)

Group Game:
Instead of "Duck, Duck, Goose," play "Cat, Cat, Cow." Encourage students to make the corresponding animal sounds when they chase one another.

Crafty Cat
(See the directions on page 20.)

Practice Page:
See page 22 for letter-recognition and sound-association practice.

Class Book:
Have each student draw something that begins with *C* on a large sheet of paper and then dictate or write a caption with a format similar to the one shown. Bind students' pages into a book titled "Camera, Camera, What Do You See?" and decorate the front cover with a camera cutout.

I see a big camel.

Songs and Such for the Week

Cool Changes
(tune: "Did You Ever See a Lassie?")

Did you ever catch a caterpillar,
A caterpillar, a caterpillar.
Did you ever catch a caterpillar and
    watch it change?
Did it spin a cocoon
One sunny afternoon?
Did you ever catch a caterpillar and
    watch it change?

Do You Know?
(tune: "The Muffin Man")

Oh, do you know that [cocoa] starts,
[Cocoa] starts, [cocoa] starts,
Oh, do you know that [cocoa] starts
With the letter *C*?

C on the Menu
Cookies are yummy;
Cake is too.
But carrots and corn
Are better for you!

Cut, Cut, Cut!

Set out a variety of paper strips. To begin, cut the strips as desired. For example, fringe-cut the edges, snip the strips into shorter pieces, or cut them into different shapes. Then glue the cut paper in a pleasing arrangement on a sheet of paper. Showcase the completed artwork with the title "*C* Is for *Cut!*"

Crafty Cat

Use arts-and-crafts materials to make a cat's face on a construction paper circle. Next, glue two paper triangles (ears) to the head and then glue the head to the top of a triangle cutout (body). Cut two smaller paper circles in half to make legs and feet and glue them to the body. Then draw two lines (legs) on the body. Finally, draw a collar and glue on a construction paper circle labeled "C."

Words

cake	camel	camera	candle	candy	cap
car	carrot	castle	cat	caterpillar	cave
coat	cocoa	computer	cookie	corn	cup

TEC61391

TEC61391

TEC61391

TEC61391

TEC61391

TEC61391

TEC61391

TEC61391

TEC61391

TEC61391

TEC61391

TEC61391

Letter recognition, sound association

I Know About C!

Color the pictures that begin like .

Circle each **Cc**.

Cc

h	c	C	f
C	F	d	c
C	c	H	C

Centers
for the Week

D Is for...

Dinosaurs and Dig: Hide plastic dinosaurs in sand in a sand table. Set out small plastic shovels, hand brooms or toothbrushes, and disposable pie pans. Invite center visitors to unearth the dinosaurs, brush them off, and put them in the pie pans.

Dots: For each student, write a large lowercase *d* and a large uppercase *D* on a sheet of white paper. Set out cotton swabs, a shallow container of white glue, and a supply of hole-punched circles (dots). A child uses a cotton swab to spread glue along the letters. Then she says, "*D* is for *dots!*" as she sprinkles dots on the glue.

Doughnuts: Get a clean and empty doughnut box. Make a supply of construction paper doughnuts. Write *D*s on most of the doughnuts. Write a different easy-to-distinguish letter on each remaining doughnut. Students put each doughnut with a *D* in the box and set aside each doughnut with a different letter.

Group Time	Literature

Monday

D is for *down*! Have students stand. Then slowly name words, one at a time, including *D* words. When a child hears a word that begins with /d/, he bends his knees and dips down. When he hears a word that does not begin with /d/, he stands upright. ***Phonemic awareness***

To follow up a read-aloud of *Dinosaurs, Dinosaurs* by Byron Barton, make two copies of page 27. Write an uppercase *D* on each dinosaur on one copy. On the other copy, write a lowercase *d* on each dinosaur. Cut apart the cards and then have students match the cards as in the traditional game of Concentration.

Tuesday

Make a class supply of dog bone cutouts. Write a letter on each bone, writing mostly *D*s. Hide the bones in the classroom. Then set out a toy stuffed dog. Have students find the bones, put the *D* bones in front of the dog, and set the other bones aside. ***Letter recognition***

The descriptive text in *Dinosaurs, Dinosaurs* is sure to inspire your young artists! Discuss with students different characteristics of dinosaurs, such as spikes and horns. Then have each child draw a dinosaur and dictate a descriptive caption for you to write.

Wednesday

Stand with students in a circle. Explain that *dance* begins with *D*. Then give students *D*-related dancing instructions. Invite them to dance like a dinosaur, a duck, a dolphin, or round and round like a doughnut. They're sure to enjoy a digging dance, a dipping dance, and a dusting dance too! ***Letter-sound association***

Before reading aloud *Duck at the Door* by Jackie Urbanovic, try this knock-knock activity. Begin by saying, "Knock, knock." After students ask, "Who's there?", name an animal. Students invite it to come in if its name begins with /d/ and ask it to return later if its name does not begin with /d/.

Thursday

For this vocabulary stretcher, highlight unfamiliar insects and animals whose names begin with /d/, such as a dragonfly, dormouse, dromedary, dachshund, and dalmatian. As you introduce each insect or animal to students, display a picture of it on a board decorated with a jumbo *D* cutout. ***Letter-sound association***

After students are familiar with *Duck at the Door*, give each child a folded sheet of paper in which you have cut a flap (door). Have her illustrate the front of the paper so it resembles a house. Then instruct her to write a *D* on the door. Finally, ask her to fold back the door and illustrate a word that begins with *D*.

Friday

Use a simple game of charades to put action words that begin with *D* in the spotlight. There's no doubt students will be eager to dig, draw, drop, dance, and dive their way through this activity! ***Letter-sound association***

This transition tip is perfect for fans of *Duck at the Door*! Display on the classroom door large *D* cutouts and student illustrations of words that begin with *D*. When a child leaves the room, ask him to say the password—a *D* word!

Art and More!

Big and Little Dots
(See the directions on page 26.)

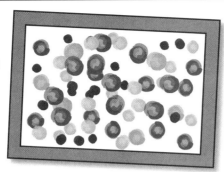

Management tip: Designate a toy stuffed dinosaur or dog as your class pet and use it as a behavior reward. Invite a good listener to sit with it at storytime, allow a student with exceptional behavior to sleep with it at naptime, or let a youngster keep it nearby as he works at centers. The possibilities are endless!

Diamond Dinosaur
(See the directions on page 26.)

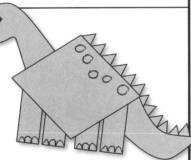

Practice Page: *See page 28 for letter-recognition and sound-association practice.*

Sarah likes chocolate doughnuts.

Class Book: Have each child draw and color his favorite type of doughnut. Then enlist his input to write a caption with a format such as "[Child's name] likes [describing word] doughnuts." Bind students' papers between two covers and title the book "Doughnuts for Dessert."

Songs and Such for the Week

Busy Doggy
(tune: "The Farmer in the Dell")

The doggy [wags its tail].
The doggy [wags its tail].
Each and every morning,
The doggy [wags its tail].

For additional verses, guide students to suggest phrases to substitute for the underlined words, such as *shakes its paw* and *chews its bone.*

Write a *D*!
(tune: "Baa, Baa, Black Sheep")

Hello, students.
Are you watching me?
I'm going to show you
How to write a *D*.

Start at the top
And come straight down.
Then lift up your pencil
And curve down and around.

Thank you, students.
You were watching me!
That is how you
Make a *D*.

D 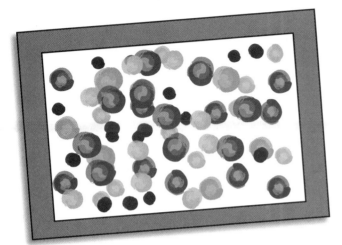 Art Activities d

Big and Little Dots

In advance, set out bingo daubers, cotton swabs, shallow containers of paint, and paper. Use the daubers and cotton swabs dipped in paint to make big and little dots on a sheet of paper. Continue until the desired effect is achieved. After the paint dries, mount the artwork on a larger piece of colored paper.

Diamond Dinosaur

Glue a cutout construction paper dinosaur head and neck to a large construction paper diamond as shown. After you draw a face, cut four paper strips to make legs and glue them to the diamond. Cut a tail and triangles from paper to make spikes and glue them along the back of the dinosaur.

D Words

deer	dentist	desk	diamond	dice	dig
dinosaur	doctor	dog	doll	dollar	dolphin
domino	door	dot	doughnut	down	duck

TEC61391

TEC61391

TEC61391

TEC61391

TEC61391

TEC61391

I Know About *D*!

Color the pictures that begin like .

Circle each **Dd**.

Dd

H	D	d	c
D	h	d	d
d	D	F	D

Centers for the Week

E Is for...

Egg: Gather a supply of identical plastic eggs. Write an uppercase *E* on the top half of each egg and a lowercase *e* on the bottom half. Open the eggs, scramble the egg halves, and then put them in a basket. Set out paper. A student puts the eggs back together and then writes uppercase and lowercase *E*s on a sheet of paper.

Envelope: Write "Ee" on one envelope and draw a sad face on a different envelope. Write an alphabet letter on each of a supply of blank index cards, including several uppercase and lowercase *E*s. Students sort the cards, putting the *E* and *e* cards in the lettered envelope and the rest of the cards in the illustrated envelope.

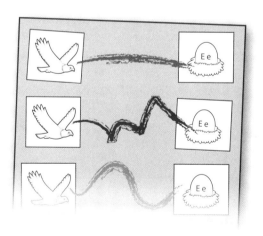

Eagle: Set out student copies of page 33, large sheets of light-colored paper, scissors, glue, cotton swabs, and a shallow container of paint. A child cuts out the picture cards from one copy. She glues the eagle cards along one long side of a paper and the nest cards along the other long side. Then she dips a cotton swab in paint and paints a straight, curvy, or zigzag path from each eagle to a different nest.

	Group Time	Literature

Monday

Put on the floor a large grid programmed with lettered peanut cutouts, including *E*s. Youngsters say the chant "Peanut Pleaser" (page 31) as each student, in turn, tosses a beanbag on the grid. If the beanbag lands on an *e*, students trumpet imaginary elephant trunks! *Letter recognition*

To follow up *First the Egg* by Laura Vaccaro Seeger, have students sit on the floor in a semicircle facing you. Roll a plastic egg to a child; have him name a story detail or make a book-related comment and then roll the egg back to you. Continue until each child has a turn.

Tuesday

Put letter cards that show mostly *E*s in an envelope. Pass the envelope around as the group chants, "*E* is for an *envelope* that we send." The student holding the envelope at the end of the chant removes a card at random. If it shows an *E*, she keeps it. If it does not, she sets it aside. Continue until the envelope is "*E* is for *empty*." *Letter recognition*

In advance, label each of a supply of egg cutouts with a letter, including mostly *E*s. To begin, read aloud *First the Egg*. Then gather students in a circle (nest) and put the eggs in the middle of the nest. Each student, in turn, pantomimes a chicken clucking as he takes an egg labeled "E."

Wednesday

Discuss with students the sounds associated with *E*. Point out that *echo* begins with *E*. Then say a word. If it begins with /ĕ/, students echo you. If it does not begin with /ĕ/, each child covers his mouth. For added fun, use a soft, deep, high, or low voice as you continue with different words. *Phonemic awareness*

Put green plastic eggs in an empty sanitized egg carton. Set out a frying pan and a bowl. After you read aloud *Green Eggs and Ham* by Dr. Seuss, a student takes an egg. He names a place to eat green eggs and then pantomimes cracking the egg into the pan. After he puts the shells in the bowl, a different student takes a turn.

Thursday

Put pairs of uppercase and lowercase letter *E* manipulatives in plastic eggs, putting one letter in each egg. Put a different letter in each of several other eggs. Spread out the eggs on cellophane grass. Students play like Concentration, pairing uppercase and lowercase *E*s and setting other eggs aside. *Letter identification*

Before reading *Green Eggs and Ham* a second time, give each student a sheet of paper and a green crayon. Have him listen carefully for the word *eggs* as you read. Each time he hears the word, he draws an egg and writes an *e* on it. At the end of the story, compare the number of eggs each child drew.

Friday

What's special about *eleven*? It starts with *E*! Students line up side by side. Then they count off from one to 11 several times. Each student who says *eleven* writes an *E* on the board and then sits down. There's no doubt youngsters will be eager to see who's the last student standing! *Letter-sound association*

...nine, ten, eleven!

Would you, could you, on a cracker? Would you eat egg salad, that is! After students are familiar with *Green Eggs and Ham*, mix a batch of egg salad and serve each student a spoonful on a cracker. Mmmm! "Eggs-cellent!"

Art and More!

Eager Elephant
(See the directions on page 32.)

Transition Tip: Invite students to stomp like elephants, slither like *eels*, or fly like *eagles* as they move from one activity to another. They're sure to develop word associations with the letter *e* and work off excess energy!

Egg Roll
(See the directions on page 32.)

Practice Page: *See page 34 for letter-recognition practice.*

Class Book: For each student, attach the front of an envelope to a sheet of paper. Each child writes "Ee" on his envelope. He draws on a blank card something that begins with *E*. Then he puts the card in the envelope. After you label the page with the name of the illustrated item, bind students' papers between two covers and title the book "What's Inside?"

Ee

elephant

Songs and Such for the Week

Peanut Pleaser
Peanuts for breakfast.
Peanuts for lunch.
This elephant likes
E peanuts to munch!

Exit Explanation
(tune: "The Mulberry Bush")

An exit is not the way in,
The way in, the way in.
An exit is not the way in.
The opposite is true.

An exit is the way out,
The way out, the way out.
An exit is the way out
Of places like the zoo!

Just Like This!
(tune: "For He's a Jolly Good Fellow")

We're writing uppercase *E*.
We're writing uppercase *E*.
We're writing uppercase *E*;
We write it just like this.

Down, across—one, two, three;
Down, across—one, two, three;
Down, across—one, two, three.
That's the letter *E*!

Eager Elephant

Cut a small, medium, and large circle from gray or light blue construction paper to make an elephant ear, head, and body, respectively. Glue the circles together as shown. Draw a face on the elephant. Then accordion-fold a narrow paper strip to make a trunk. Unfold the strip and glue one end to the head. To make legs, cut four rectangles from construction paper and glue them in place. Then tape a length of yarn to the elephant to make a tail.

Egg Roll

In advance, set out small bowls containing paint and put a plastic spoon in each. Use a loop of tape to secure a sheet of white paper in a shallow box. Put a few spoonfuls of paint on the paper and then roll a few plastic eggs through the paint. Continue until a desired effect is achieved. Then remove the eggs and paper. After the paint dries, cut an egg shape from the paper.

E Words

eagle	ear	eat	edge	eel	egg
electric	elephant	elevator	eleven	elf	end
envelope	eraser	every	excellent	exit	extra

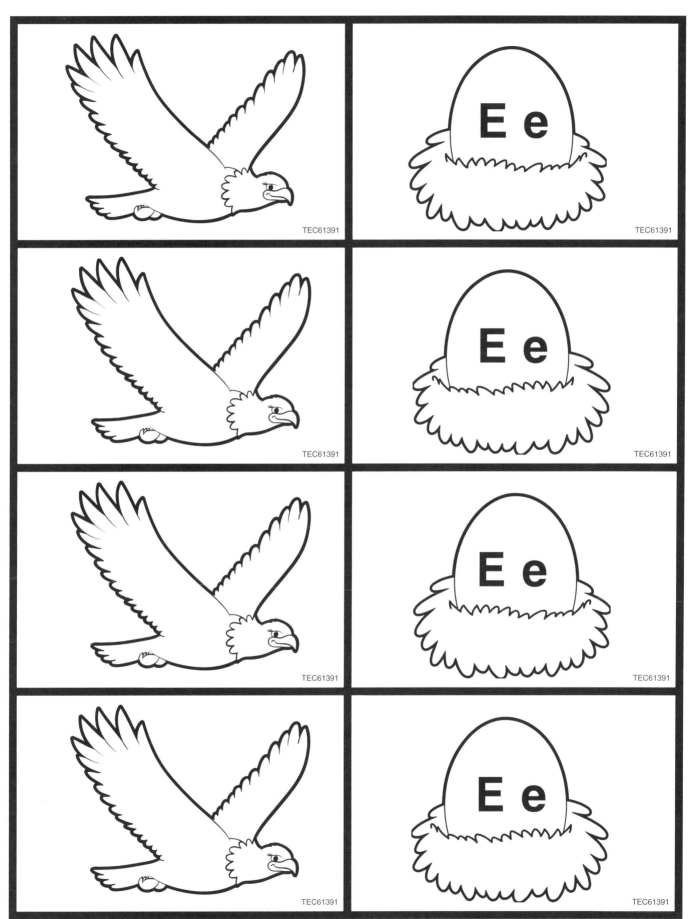

TEC61391

E e

TEC61391

TEC61391

E e

TEC61391

TEC61391

E e

TEC61391

TEC61391

E e

TEC61391

Name _____

I Can Find *E*!

✏️ Circle.

E

E	e	C
e	h	D	E

e h D E

d e E H

E c e

Centers for the Week

F Is for...

Fish: Cut simple fish shapes from craft foam. Use a permanent marker to write *F* on both sides of several cutouts and letters other than *F* on the remaining cutouts. Float the fish shapes in your water table. Provide a child-size fishing net and a plastic bucket. A child chants, "Here fishy, fishy!" as he uses the fishing net to scoop out fish labeled *F*.

Footprints: For this matching activity, label pairs of footprint cutouts with *F* and *f*. Place the cutouts at a center. A student makes pairs of footprints by matching each uppercase *F* to a lowercase *f*. For added fun, stock the center with shoeboxes. Each time a youngster makes a match, she puts the pair in a box.

Feather: Pour a mixture of sand and fine glitter (for a bit of sparkle) in a tray or shallow tub. Also provide colorful craft feathers and a letter formation card for *F* and *f*. A youngster uses the sturdy end of a craft feather for letter-writing practice.

Group Time	Literature
Monday Give each child a craft feather to hold in her lap. Say the word *feather* and have students listen carefully for the /f/ sound. Repeat with the word *fancy*. Then say different words, encouraging students to wave their fancy feathers in the air when a word begins with /f/ and keep their fancy feathers in their laps when it does not. ***Beginning sounds***	Take students on a colorful fish fantasy! Read aloud *Fish Eyes: A Book You Can Count On* by Lois Ehlert. Invite students to compare Ehlert's colorful fish to other fish they've seen. Then find out why students think the author chose the title she did. 
Tuesday On a wall, arrange paper rectangles and paper logs to make a fireplace. For each child, label opposite ends of a paper flame with a different letter, making one letter *F* (or *f*). Hide the cutouts. Ask each child to find a cutout and hold it so the *F* is at the top. To make a cozy classroom fire, tape each flame inside the fireplace so only the letter *F* can be seen. ***Letter recognition*** 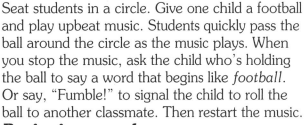	Have each child color a simple fish pattern. Help her cut out the fish and attach it to a jumbo craft stick. Invite students to bring their fish puppets to a second oral reading of *Fish Eyes: A Book You Can Count On*. As you read, hold each beginning /f/ sound, signaling students to raise their fish puppets in response.
Wednesday Seat students in a circle. Give one child a football and play upbeat music. Students quickly pass the ball around the circle as the music plays. When you stop the music, ask the child who's holding the ball to say a word that begins like *football*. Or say, "Fumble!" to signal the child to roll the ball to another classmate. Then restart the music. ***Beginning sounds***	Read aloud *The Foot Book* by Dr. Seuss. Ask each child to point to his feet, touch his face, and wiggle his fingers. Emphasize the /f/ sound in the name of each body part. Then assist students in counting the number of feet, faces, and fingers in the classroom! Also invite each child to find out how many feet are in his family for tomorrow's activity. 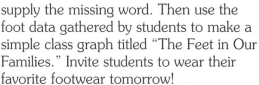
Thursday Write letters on the board, including several *F*s. Have students take turns pretending to be a fish, "swimming" to the board, and circling an *F*. When each *F* is circled, erase the letters and write another set. ***Letter identification***	Reread yesterday's story. During this oral reading, pause each time the word *feet* appears, and have students supply the missing word. Then use the foot data gathered by students to make a simple class graph titled "The Feet in Our Families." Invite students to wear their favorite footwear tomorrow!
Friday Fireflies come out during this activity! Display a letter *F* sign. Announce a word. Ask the group to decide whether the word begins with /f/. If it does, the students say /f/ and then make a buzzing sound while fluttering their fingers in the air. If it does not, the youngsters do nothing. Repeat the activity with different words. ***Letter-sound association***	A footwear parade is a perfect finale for a final reading of *The Foot Book*! Have students sit along both sides of a paper runway. In two or three places along the path, write "Ff." To model her footwear, a student struts down the runway, pausing at each letter pair to show off her feet!

Art and More!

Fork Art
(See the directions on page 38.)

Gross Motor: Have students hold hands to form two lines, or *fences*, facing each other. To take a turn, the members of one team raise their joined hands and chant, "Fee, fie, foe, fum, join our fence for lots of fun!" Call on one or more children from the opposing team to march, jog, or tiptoe through the fence line and join the team. Keep playing until every student has switched teams one or more times.

F Is for Fox
(See the directions on page 38.)

Practice Page: *See page 40 for letter-recognition practice.*

Class Book: To make the first booklet page, write "If We Could Be Fish…" To make each remaining page, have each student draw the fish he would like to be and dictate a caption for you to write. Bind the completed pages between two covers.

Jared would be a famous fish.

Songs and Such for the Week

If I Could Be a Fishy
(tune: "Did You Ever See a Lassie?")

If I could be a fishy,
A fishy, a fishy,
If I could be a fishy,
What kind would I be?
Would I be a [farm] fish?
A [football] fish?
A [fork] fish?
If I could be a fishy,
What kind would I be?

Continue with the following:
feather, fancy, fire, fuzzy, famous, funny, and other words that begin with /f/.

All About *F*
(tune: "Are You Sleeping?")

F says /f/.
F says /f/.
F for *fin*,
F for *feet*.
I can make the letter *f*.
I can make the letter *f*,
And that is super neat!

Suggestion: Encourage students to write the letter in the air as they say the fifth and sixth lines of the rhyme.

F Art Activities

Fork Art

Grab a plastic fork, a sheet of white construction paper, and four colors of tempera paint, and you're ready to make fork art! Put a dollop of each paint color in a different corner of the paper. Then use the fork to spread and swirl the paint, blending the colors as you go until a desired outcome is achieved.

F Is for Fox

Cut a 5" x 8" rectangle (body) and a seven-inch semicircle (head) from brown construction paper. Also cut out a brown construction paper copy of the patterns on page 39. Sponge white paint on the facial fur and tail cutouts and set them aside to dry. Add construction paper or crayon details to the cutouts and then assemble the pieces to make the fox shown. Put paper shreds in the bottom of a brown paper lunch bag, fold back the top inch of the bag, and tape the bag closed. Glue the fox to the front of the bag to finish this self-standing project.

F Words

face	fan	farm	feast	feather	feet
fence	fin	fingers	fire	fish	foil
food	foot	fork	fort	fox	fur

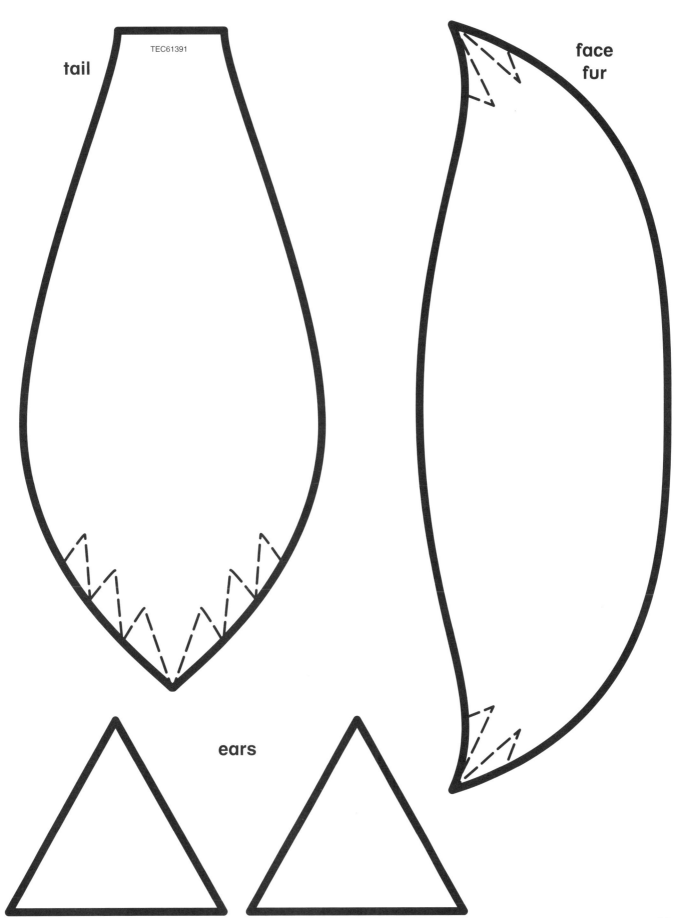

tail

TEC61391

face
fur

ears

I Can Find *F*!

 Circle.

F

s	K	f
a	f	r	F
b	F	D	R
F	f	C	

Day-by-Day Alphabet Plans • ©The Mailbox® Books • TEC61391

Centers
for the Week

G Is for...

Gumball: Make a class supply of page 45. A student colors each gumball that is labeled with a *G*. Or, if desired, place a sheet of colorful round stickers at the center along with the reproducibles. The student covers each *G* gumball with a sticker.

Gold: Label each of several construction paper sheets with a large *G*. Also paint a supply of medium-size rocks or pebbles with gold paint. After the paint dries, label each rock with a *G* and place the rocks (gold) in a basket or bowl. To reinforce letter formation and identification skills, a student places the pieces of gold on one of the letter outlines.

Gift: Cut out a matching supply of paper squares and simple bow shapes from colorful paper. Label each square (gift) with an uppercase *G* and each bow with a lowercase *g*. Store the cutouts in a small gift bag. The student removes the cutouts from the bag and sorts them into gifts and bows. Then she places each bow atop a gift.

	Group Time	Literature
Monday	Label cards with uppercase letters, labeling most with a *G*. Place the cards faceup in your group area, along with a pot and a spoon. Recite "*G* Gumbo" on page 43. A student volunteer finds a *G* card and tosses it in the pot. Continue until all *G* cards are in the pot. ***Letter identification***	Give each student a card labeled with a *G*. Tell students that the story you will read is about a sneaky gorilla, and that *gorilla* starts with *G*. Then read aloud *Good Night, Gorilla* by Peggy Rathmann. Have each student hold up his card and quietly say, "/g/, /g/, /g/" each time he sees the gorilla on a page. 
Tuesday	Draw a triangle on the board. Announce two words: one that begins with /g/ and one that does not. Ask a student to identify which word begins with /g/ like *goat*. Then have him add a detail to the triangle, such as an ear, a nose, an eye, a horn, or whiskers. Continue until the triangle has been transformed into a cute goat. ***Beginning sounds***	Reread yesterday's story. Then have students stand. Say, "Good night, [word]." If the word begins with /g/, each student pretends to tiptoe quietly like the gorilla in the story. If it does not, the student stands still.
Wednesday	Point out to students that *goose* starts with /g/. Then play a version of "Duck, Duck, Goose," but have a student replace *duck* with a word that starts with /g/, such as "*game, game, goose.*" Encourage students to help another youngster identify a different /g/ word for the next round. ***Beginning sounds***	After reading *Goldilocks and the Three Bears* by Jan Brett, place picture cards (mostly *G* words) and a gift bag in your group area. Explain that Goldilocks could have given the bears a gift to apologize for her actions. Then have each child choose a picture that begins with *G*, like *gift*, and drop the card in the gift bag.
Thursday	Label a large piece of green paper (putting green) with one *G* for each student plus a few extra letters. Place a class supply of paper golf balls, each labeled with a *G*, around the room in easy-to-find locations. Each child finds a ball and, in turn, places it atop a *G* on the putting green. ***Letter identification*** 	Reread yesterday's story. Compare the sizes of the bears and their household items (little, middle-size, huge). Then have students sort a collection of small, medium, and large cards that are each labeled with a *G*.
Friday	Label paper scraps with letters (mostly *G*s). Crumple the scraps and place them in your group area. A student (the garbage collector) picks up a scrap and reads its letter. If it is labeled with a *G*, the student says, "Garbage!" and tosses the scrap in a trash can. If it is not, he drops it back in the group area. Continue until all *G*s have been collected. ***Letter recognition***	Have each child spread honey-flavored butter in the shape of a *G* on a slice of toast. Add two banana slice ears and a banana slice nose. Then add blueberry eyes. Before he eats the snack, prompt him to say, "/g/, /g/, good!"

Art and More!

Golden Tissue Painting
(See the directions on page 44.)

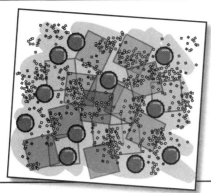

Practice Page: *See page 46 for letter-identification and sound-association practice.*

Garden Gates
(See the directions on page 44.)

Transition Tip: To reinforce the /g/ sound, call students to line up or to go to group activities using the words *gals* and *guys*.

Class Book: Ask each child to draw a picture of a garden. Then have her place several sticky dots labeled with a *G* on her picture. Bind the pictures behind a cover labeled with the chant "This Is Our Garden" found to the right.

Songs and Such for the Week

It Begins With G!
(tune: Row, Row, Row Your Boat")

Teacher: /g/, /g/, what do you see
That begins with G?
Children: A [gate], a [gate] is what we see.
A [gate] begins with G!

Have children choose a different G word for each verse.

G Gumbo

Cooking up some gumbo
Till it's nice and hot!
Looking for a yummy G
To toss into the pot!

This Is Our Garden

This is our garden,
As you can see.
We're growing something special.
Can you find each G?

 # Art Activities

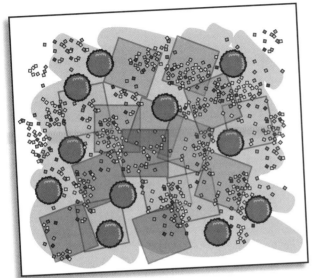

Golden Tissue Painting

Gather gold paint, tissue paper, pom-poms, and glitter. Then paint a sheet of paper and attach items as desired. This masterpiece is a treasure!

Garden Gates

Glue seven craft sticks together to make a gate as shown. Then glue the gate to construction paper, leaving room at the top. Next, glue green paper strips (stems) to the gate and attach torn paper scraps to the tops of the stems so they resemble flowers. Write "[Your name]'s Garden Gate" at the top of the paper and underline the Gs.

G Words

game	garage	garbage	gas	gate	get
gift	girl	give	goal	goat	gold
golf	goose	gorilla	got	guitar	gum

Gumball Machine Pattern

Use with "Gumball" on page 41.

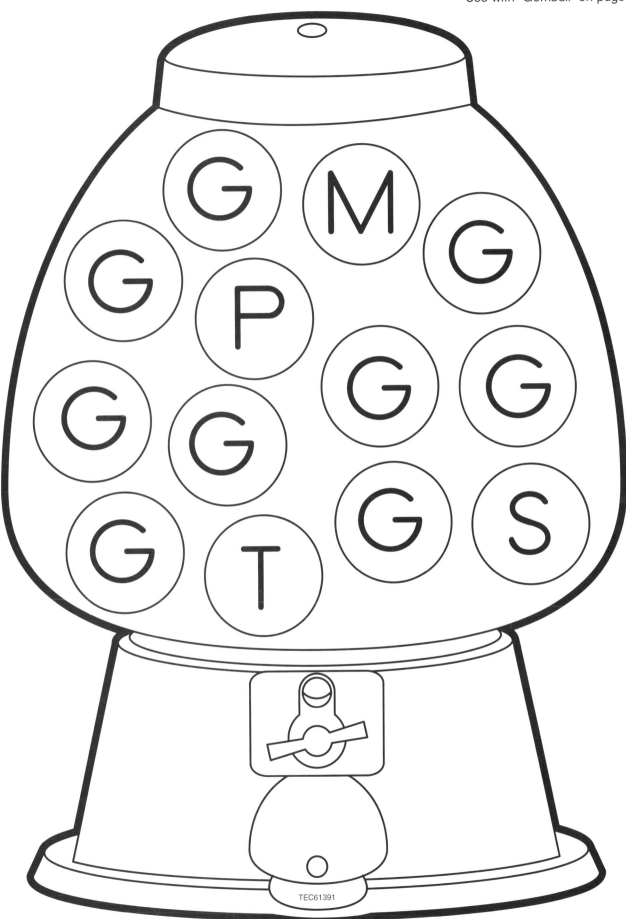

TEC61391

Day-by-Day Alphabet Plans • ©The Mailbox® Books • TEC61391

45

Letter recognition, sound association

I Know About G!

Color the pictures that begin like .

Circle each **Gg**.

Gg

p	G	g	s
S	P	g	G
T	G	g	g

Day-by-Day Alphabet Plans • ©The Mailbox® Books • TEC61391

Centers
for the Week

H Is for...

Houses: For this house-building center, cut from construction paper eight squares and two triangles (roofs). Write "H" on one triangle and four squares. Write "h" on the remaining cutouts. Put the labeled shapes at a center. A student uses the cutouts to build an uppercase *H* and a lowercase *h* house.

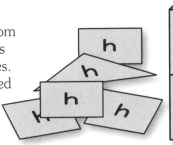
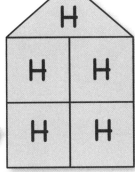

Helicopter: Cut apart a copy of the beginning sound cards on page 51 and glue each one to a large circle cutout. Add desired details to the resulting helipads and then put them at a center along with a toy helicopter. A student flies and lands the toy helicopter, naming the picture on a helipad before the helicopter touches down on it.

Hopping: Use masking tape to form a large *H* and *h* on the floor. To reinforce letter identification, invite students to chant the name of the letters as they hop around the shapes. For letter-sound association practice, have students chant, "*H* says /h/" as they hop. To reinforce beginning sounds, ask students to name words that begin with /h/!

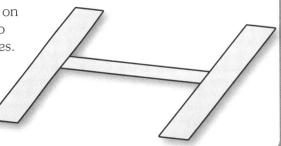

Group Time	Literature

Monday

Arrange students in a large circle around a haystack cutout (or yellow paper scraps). Ask each child to mount an imaginary horse. Tell students to listen to the beginning sound of each word you announce. When a word begins like *hay*, they may ride their horses to the haystack and back! ***Beginning sounds***

Collect several hats and a few random items. Have each child place an *H* card on each item he thinks is a hat. When all the hats have *H*s, explain that the hen you're going to read about thinks that many different things can be a hat! Read aloud *A Hat for Minerva Louise* by Janet Morgan Stoeke.

Tuesday

Label each of several blank cards with a letter, writing *H* on most. Hold a card in the air. If the letter on the card is *H*, students hum, hoot, howl, or honk. If it is not, the youngsters sit quietly. ***Letter recognition***

Invite students to bring hats from home for today's oral reading. After your rereading, announce words, some that begin like *hat* and some that do not. Invite students to tip their hats each time they hear the beginning sound /h/!

Wednesday

For this Concentration game, write *H* and *h* on opposite halves of several die-cut hearts. Cut the shapes in half and arrange them facedown on a tabletop. Gather students around the table. Each child takes a turn flipping two heart halves. When a letter pair is found, the mended heart is set aside and the group chants, "Happy heart!" Play until all hearts are mended. ***Uppercase and lowercase letters***

At your easel, draw an outline of a house. Label the drawing "*H* Is for *House*." Have students suggest ways to perk up the house, such as adding a colorful door or curtained windows. Then read aloud *A House for Hermit Crab* by Eric Carle to learn how a crab perks up his new house!

Thursday

Cut three strips that make an uppercase *H* from each of several colors of paper. Put the strips inside a Happy Hippo bag. Each child takes one strip from the bag. Then he works with two classmates to make a solid color uppercase *H*. If strips remain in the bag, distribute them to the proper group(s). Verify the letters; then collect the strips and play again. ***Letter formation***

In advance, draw a large shell shape on bulletin board paper. Label the drawing "Hermit Crab's New House." Reread yesterday's story. Tell students that Hermit Crab has decided to decorate his newest home with objects whose names begin with the sound /h/. Invite them to brainstorm what those objects might be!

Friday

The letter *H* is hiding! Place a cut-apart copy of the beginning sound cards (page 51) faceup in a pocket chart. Hide a letter *H* card behind one picture. Invite a child to name a picture. When she does, move its card to see whether the *H* is hiding there. Continue until the *H* is found. To play again, vary the placement of all cards. ***Letter-sound association***

Cut apart a copy of the picture cards from page 51. Put the cards and desired distracter cards in a sand pail. Remind students of Hermit Crab's decorating plan from yesterday's story and point to the labeled shell shape. Invite each child to take a picture from the pail, name it, and decide (with his classmates' help) whether to glue it to "Hermit Crab's New House."

Art and More!

Handy Hammer Prints
(See the directions on page 50.)

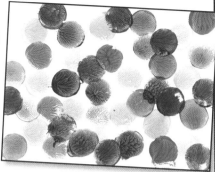

Gross Motor: Increase your youngsters' heart rates with an aerobic workout! Use "Letter *H* Aerobics" on this page as your guide. Recite each verse, allowing time for students to complete the described actions.

Heart-to-Heart Headbands
(See the directions on page 50.)

Practice Page: *See page 52 for letter-recognition practice.*

Class Book: Each child glues a paper lowercase *h* on paper. She transforms the letter into a horse by drawing a head, ears, mane, and tail. Next, she adds details and dictates a caption. Bind the completed pages together with a cover titled "Our Herd of Horses!"

My horse has spots. She eats hay. Her name is Holly.

Songs and Such for the Week

Hooray for *H*!
(tune: "Mary Had a Little Lamb")

[Horse] starts with the letter *H*,
The letter *H*, the letter *H*.
[Horse] starts with the letter *H*,
And *H* sounds like this—/h/!

Letter *H* Aerobics

Clap your hands.
Hop around.
Head up high.
Feet off the ground.

Clap your hands.
Ride a horse.
Hold your hat.
Stay on course.

Clap your hands.
Hike a hill.
Feel your heart.
Then stand still.

Clap your hands.
Stomp your heels.
Hands on hips.
How do you feel?

Art Activities

Handy Hammer Prints

Prepare two or more shallow containers with different colors of paint. You will also need a container of rinse water, a toy hammer, and construction paper. To make a print, dip the hammer in a pan of paint, gently tap the hammer on the paper one or more times, and then repeat. To switch paint colors, rinse the hammer in the water. Continue the process until a desired outcome is achieved.

Heart-to-Heart Headbands

Precut one headband-size paper strip per child and cut a variety of heart shapes from construction paper, foam, and gift wrap. Also provide glue, markers, and tape. To make a headband, choose several heart shapes and use a marker to label each one with *H* or *h*. Then cover a section of the paper strip with glue and press hearts on the glue. Repeat the gluing process until the strip is decorated. Tape the ends of the strip together to complete the headband.

H Words

hair	hall	hammer	hand	happy	hat
hay	head	heart	heel	hen	hill
hole	honey	hook	hop	horn	horse

TEC61391

TEC61391

TEC61391

TEC61391

TEC61391

TEC61391

TEC61391

TEC61391

TEC61391

TEC61391

TEC61391

TEC61391

I Can Find H!

 Circle.

H

u	H	m
t	B	h	H
h	P	H	d
b	h	E	h

Day-by-Day Alphabet Plans • ©The Mailbox® Books • TEC61391

Centers for the Week

I Is for...

Inside: To make four observation bottles, label both sides of four craft foam squares with an uppercase *I* or a lowercase *i*. Put each foam square into a different clear plastic bottle. Add to each container itty-bitty items, such as sand, rice, or beans; then hot-glue a lid on each one. Shake each bottle until its letter is out of sight. A student shakes, tilts, and rolls each bottle to find the *I* or *i* that's hiding in the itty-bitty items.

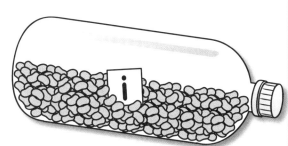

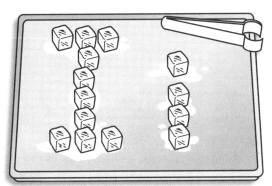

Ice: Put at a center a small Styrofoam cooler, a tray with raised edges, alphabet cards for *I* and *i,* and a pair of tongs or garden-type gloves. Stock the cooler with ice cubes. A child wears the gloves or uses the tongs to move several ice cubes from the cooler to the tray. Then she arranges the cubes to form an *I* or *i*. Encourage students to observe how the ice on the tray changes as they work.

Ice Cream: For this partner game, prepare four ice cream cone cutouts and 12 ice cream scoop cutouts. Label half the cones and scoops with an uppercase *I*. Label the remaining cutouts with a lowercase *i*. To begin, partners place the scoops facedown and take one of each cone type. In turn, each student flips a scoop and puts it on his matching cone. When every scoop is part of a cone, the players compare the treats they've made.

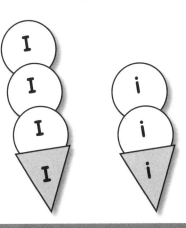

	Group Time	Literature
Monday	Play Ivan Says. Students stand shoulder to shoulder on a starting line and pretend to be wearing ice skates. When Ivan says a word that begins like *ice*, each child skates forward one step. When Ivan says a word that doesn't begin like *ice*, students stand still. When a child moves incorrectly, he skates back to the starting line. **Beginning sounds**	Lead students in saying *itsy* several times, listening for the sound of short /i/. Ask them what they think the word means. Read aloud *The Itsy Bitsy Spider* by Iza Trapani and then revisit the meaning of *itsy* as needed.
Tuesday	Gather students in a circle and give each child two stick puppets: one for *I* and one for *i*. Use the lyrics from "Big and Little I" on page 55 to lead students in moving their letter puppets as indicated. **Reinforcing letter names**	In advance, draw a simple spiderweb on paper. Title the web "Itsy Items!" Collect small objects that can be glued or taped to the web. Reread *The Itsy Bitsy Spider*. Invite each child to choose an itsy item and then help him attach it to the web. Be sure to include an itsy-bitsy plastic spider!
Wednesday	Cut apart a copy of the cards on page 57. Seat students around an island-shaped cutout. Place the cards facedown around the island. To take a turn, a child selects a card, names the picture, and shows it to his classmates. If the name of the picture begins like *island*, he puts the card on the island. If not, he hands the card to you. **Beginning sounds**	Read aloud *Inch by Inch* by Leo Lionni. Give each child a 1" x 4" strip of green construction paper. Show students how to use their paper inchworms to mimic the moves of the story's main character. Invite students to inch their inchworms around the classroom while saying, "My itsy inchworm is inching along."
Thursday	Give each child a bingo dauber and a paper showing a large outline of an uppercase *I*. Say different words, many of which begin with short /i/. Pause after each word. When a word begins with a short /i/, such as *insect*, a child says, "[*Insect*] begins like *ink*!" and puts a daub of ink inside his letter outline. When a word does not begin like *ink*, he does nothing. **Letter-sound association**	Reread *Inch by Inch*. Return the students' paper inchworms from yesterday or hand out a new set. Help the youngsters arrange the inchworms on a length of bulletin board paper to form an *I* and *i*. Glue the worms in place, dotting the *i* with a green marker or circle cutout. *I* and *i* are for *inchworm*!
Friday	Draw the outline of a large glass on chart paper. Inside the outline, write uppercase *I*s and lowercase *i*'s and a few other letters. Display the paper within student reach. Invite students to find and identify each *I* and *i* and draw an ice cube around it. **Letter identification**	Give each child a construction paper strip sized to make a child's wristband. Ask each child to draw an itsy-bitsy spider and a green inchworm near the center of his paper strip; then tape the ends of his project together. Suggest that he wear his wristband home and tell his family each main character's story.

Art and More!

Sparkly Icicles
(See the directions on page 56.)

Gross Motor: Go to an open area for a game of icicle tag. A volunteer is the sun. All other players are icicles. When the sun touches a classmate, the classmate leaves the playing area and melts to the floor. After a bit of play, say "Freeze!" Replace the sun with another volunteer and then restart the game with all players.

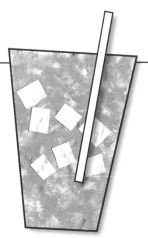

Ice-Cold Lemonade
(See the directions on page 56.)

Practice Page: *See page 58 for letter-recognition practice.*

Class Book: Give each child a prepared booklet page like the one shown. Have her write her name in the top box and draw her self-likeness in the bottom box. Bind the pages together with a cover titled "We Are Important!"

My name is
Myleah

I am important!

Songs and Such for the Week

Listen for *I*
(tune: "Where Is Thumbkin?")

Listen for /ī/. Listen for /ī/.
Say *island*. Say *ivy*.
Do you hear the /ī/ sound?
Do you hear the /ī/ sound?
/ī/ /ī/ /ī/, /ī/ /ī/ /ī/.

Listen for /ĭ/. Listen for /ĭ/.
Say *ick, ick!* Say *itch, itch!*
Do you hear the /ĭ/ sound?
Do you hear the /ĭ/ sound?
/ĭ/ /ĭ/ /ĭ/, /ĭ/ /ĭ/ /ĭ/.

Big and Little *I*
Put the big *I* in.
Take the big *I* out.
Put the big *I* in, and we give a shout.
It's an uppercase *I*, oh yes sirree!
That's an uppercase *I*, I see.

Put the little *i* in.
Take the little *i* out.
Put the little *i* in, and we give a shout.
It's a lowercase *i*, oh yes sirree!
That's a lowercase *i*, I see.

Art Activities

Sparkly Icicles

These icicles form like real ones—only much faster! Lay a half sheet of dark-colored construction paper on a paper-covered surface. Use a spoon or turkey baster to form a line of thinned white paint along one long edge of the construction paper. Next, carefully pick up the paper, keeping the paint at the top, and watch the paint roll down the paper. Then lay the paper flat and shake iridescent glitter on the icicle look-alikes. Showcase the finished projects as bulletin board border!

Ice-Cold Lemonade

This two-day project is irresistible and refreshing! On day one, fingerpaint using pink or yellow paint. On day two, trace a glass-shaped template on the back of the painted paper. Cut along the outline. Also snip several rectangles (ice cubes) from waxed paper. Glue the ice cubes to the painted surface and then glue a thin paper strip (straw) in place. Slurp!

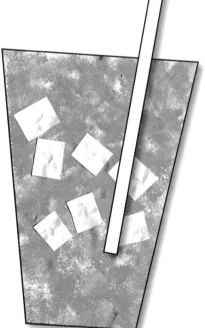

I Words

ice	iceberg	ice cream	ice skate	icicle	ick
if	igloo	iguana	in	inchworm	ink
insect	iron	island	itch	itsy	ivy

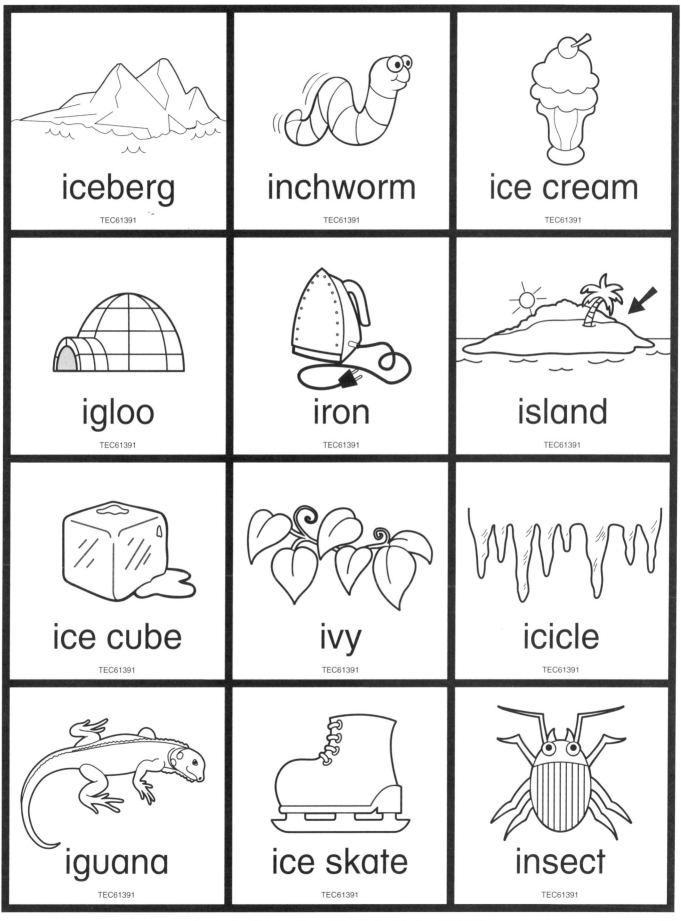

iceberg

TEC61391

inchworm

TEC61391

ice cream

TEC61391

igloo

TEC61391

iron

TEC61391

island

TEC61391

ice cube

TEC61391

ivy

TEC61391

icicle

TEC61391

iguana

TEC61391

ice skate

TEC61391

insect

TEC61391

I Can Find *I*!

✏ Circle.

I

I	x	i	j
T	i	I	M
p	Z	i	I
I	f	L	i

Day-by-Day Alphabet Plans • ©The Mailbox® Books • TEC61391

Centers
for the Week

J Is for...

Jingle: Place a jingle bell in each of several lidded, opaque containers, such as margarine tubs or coffee cans. Leave a few containers empty. Hot-glue the lids in place. A child shakes each container, softly saying "/j/ is for *jingle*." If she hears a jingle, she places the container on a paper mat labeled with a large *J*. If she doesn't hear a jingle, she sets the container aside. ***Beginning sounds***

/j/ is for *jingle*.

Jelly Bean: Label colorful jelly bean cutouts with the letter *J*, programming a few extras with different letters. A child places the jelly beans facedown. He turns over a jelly bean. If it is labeled with a *J*, he places it in a bowl. If it is labeled with a different letter, he leaves it faceup. ***Letter identification***

Jack-o'-lantern: Program a supply of cards with the letter *J*. A student takes a card and traces the letter with a crayon, saying "/j/ is for *jack-o'-lantern*" as she works. Then she drops the card into a plastic jack-o'-lantern candy bucket. She continues until she has traced five cards. ***Letter formation***

	Group Time	**Literature**
Monday	Write a list of action words or phrases, most of which begin with *J*, such as *jump, juggle, jiggle, jog*, and *jump rope*. Use the words to play a version of Simon Says called JoJo Says. When students hear a direction that begins with *J*, they perform the action. If they don't, they stand still. ***Beginning sounds***	After reading *Jamberry* by Bruce Degen, give each student a blue or red pom-pom (berry). Say the second rhyme on page 61. A child draws a card (page 63) and says its name. If the name starts with /j/, he drops his berry into a jar. If it doesn't, he sets the card aside.
Tuesday	Use jump ropes to make several large circles on the floor. Hold up a letter card. Youngsters jump into a jump rope circle if the card is labeled with a *J* and stand still if the card is not. ***Letter recognition***	After rereading *Jamberry*, gather children around a paper mat labeled with letters, including several *J*s. Give each child a small cup of colorful berry-shaped cereal. In turn, a child places a cereal piece (jamberry) on a *J* as he says, "*Jamberry* begins with /j/." When all *J*s are covered, children eat the rest of their jamberries.
Wednesday	Place a pair of jeans on the floor. Stack the cards on page 63 facedown beside the jeans. A child draws a card and shows the picture to the group. If the picture begins with /j/, the child places the card on the jeans. If not, she sets the card aside. ***Beginning sounds***	Read *Jump, Frog, Jump!* by Robert Kalan. Place a paper lily pad on the floor and scatter copies of the cards on page 63 on it. A child hops over the lily pad as the other youngsters chant, "Jump, frog, jump!" He takes a card, hops back over the lily pad, and tells whether the picture begins with /j/.
Thursday	Draw a half circle (jellyfish) on the board. Say a word that begins with /j/ and another that does not. A student volunteer determines which word begins with /j/ like *jellyfish*. Then he adds a detail to the half circle, such as a facial feature or tentacle. Continue until the half circle has been changed into a cute jellyfish. ***Beginning sounds***	Before rereading *Jump, Frog, Jump!*, label a class supply of index cards with *J*. Tape the cards to the floor. Each child sits near a card, holding a green pom-pom (frog). As you read the story aloud, whenever he hears the phrase "Jump, frog, jump," the student "jumps" his frog over his letter *J*.
Friday	On the floor, place a bottle or jar of jelly and a supply of cards, each labeled with a *J* or *j*. Include a few cards labeled with other letters. Students join hands and circle around the jelly while singing "Jelly Jig" on page 61, filling in the blank with a child's name. That child finds a pair of matching uppercase and lowercase letters and places them aside. ***Letter recognition, uppercase and lowercase letters***	To follow up *Jump, Frog, Jump!*, each child uses a craft stick to spread blue-tinted cream cheese on a graham cracker (pond). He tops the cracker with four green M&M's Minis candies (frogs), saying "/j/, /j/, jump!" as he places each candy on the pond.

Art and More!

Jazzy Jellyfish
(See the directions on page 62.)

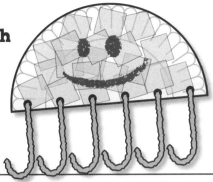

Practice Page: *See page 64 for letter-recognition practice.*

Sugar-Painted Jelly Beans
(See the directions on page 62.)

Gross-Motor: Label several beanbags with a *J*. Set a laundry basket a few feet away. A child tosses the beanbags into the basket as she practices making the /j/ sound.

Class Book: Each child dips the rim of a small paper cup in paint. He prints the cup rim on paper to make a large *J*. When the paint dries, the child colors in areas created by the overlapping circles. Bind the pages to create a class book titled "*J* Journal."

Songs and Such for the Week

Jelly Jig
(Tune: "Ring Around the Rosie")

Ring around the jelly,
Jig-a-jig-a-jelly,
[Child's name, child's name], find a pair.

J Is for *Jamberry*

J is for *jamberry*,
Berries near and far.
Find more *J* berries
To add to the jar.

Jam and Jelly

Jiggle, wiggle jelly,
Jumpy, lumpy jam.
Spread some on your toast.
Have some with your ham.
Just a jar for breakfast,
Another jar for lunch.
Jiggle jelly, jumpy jam,
Just the snack to munch!

Art Activities

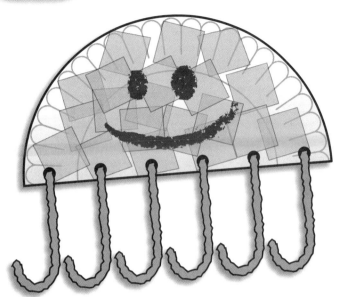

Jazzy Jellyfish

Cut a paper plate in half. Glue small squares of waxed paper on each side of the plate half. Next, punch six holes across the straight edge of the plate half. Bend each of six long pipe cleaners into a *J* shape. Thread each pipe cleaner *J* through a hole and twist to hold in place. If desired, use a glitter pen to add jazzy details to the jellyfish.

Sugar-Painted Jelly Beans

Combine sugar and several drops of food coloring with enough water to create a thick but paintable mixture. Repeat until you have several colors of sugar paint. Give each child a large jelly bean shape cut from construction paper. Each child fingerpaints his cutout using the sugar paint of his choice. Let the projects dry overnight.

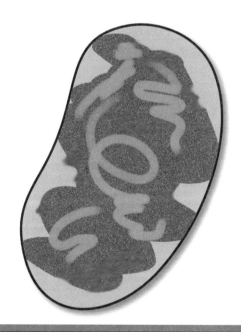

J Words

jacket	jam	jar	jaw	jeans	jeep
jelly	jellyfish	jet	jingle	job	jog
joke	joy	juice	jump	jungle	junk

Use with Wednesday's group-time activity and Monday's and Wednesday's literature activities on page 60.

TEC61391

TEC61391

TEC61391

TEC61391

TEC61391

TEC61391

TEC61391

TEC61391

TEC61391

TEC61391

TEC61391

TEC61391

I Can Find J!

✏️ Circle.

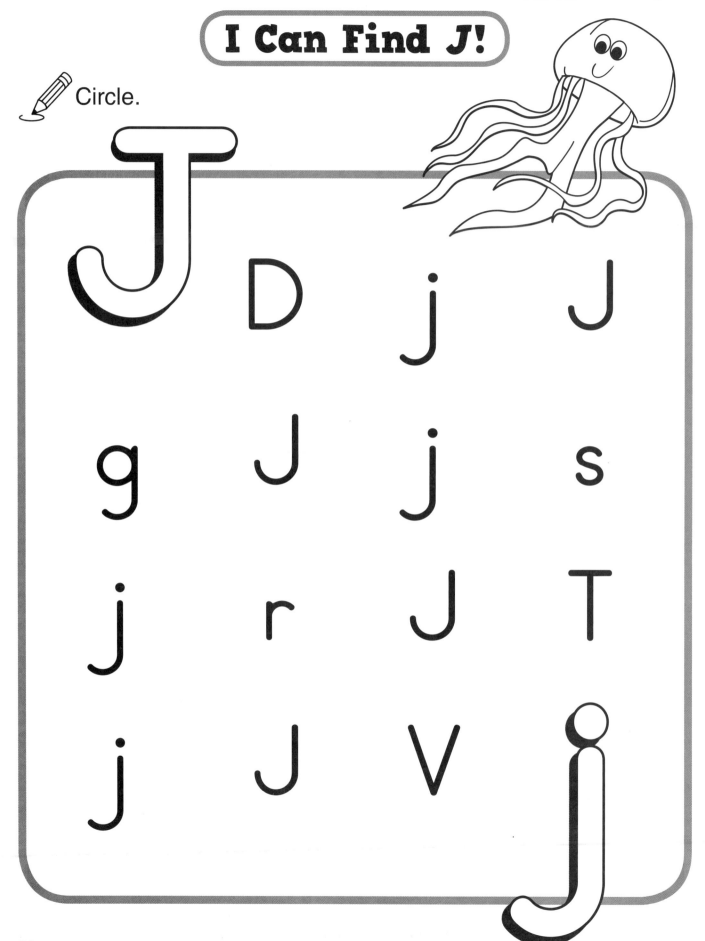

J	D	j	J
g	J	j	s
j	r	J	T
j	J	V	

 Day-by-Day Alphabet Plans • ©The Mailbox® Books • TEC61391

Centers for the Week

K Is for...

Kangaroo: Program a supply of cards with the letter *K*. Tape the cards to your floor to form a trail. A student pretends to be a kangaroo and hops along the kangaroo's trail, saying "/k/, /k/, /k/" as he hops. ***Beginning sounds***

Key: Cut out two copies of the cards on page 69. Discard cards that show items not starting with *K*. Glue each remaining card to an index card. A pair of children uses the cards to play a game of Concentration. Each time a child turns over a card, he says, "[Item's name] starts with /k/." If the two cards match, he keeps both cards. Whoever wins more pairs of cards wins the keys to the kingdom! ***Beginning sounds***

Kick: Label a set of index cards with various letters (one per card), making sure most of the letters are *K*. Stack the cards facedown at a center. A student turns over the top card. If he turns over a *K* card, he pretends to kick a ball as he softly says, "/k/ is for *kick*!" ***Letter identification***

/K/ is for kick!

	Group Time	Literature
Monday	Fill a cloth bag (pouch) with magnetic letters, most of which are *K*s. Tell students that Mama Kangaroo needs to find all her baby *k*s, but they are mixed in with other letters in her pouch. A student closes his eyes and reaches in the pouch to get a letter. If it is a *K*, he and the other students hop like kangaroos. If not, they stand still. ***Letter recognition***	Program three pairs of mitten cutouts with *K* and three additional pairs with other letters. Hide the mittens around your classroom. Read *Three Little Kittens* by Paul Galdone; then have students look to find the 12 missing mittens. Help students identify the kittens' mittens (the ones labeled with *K*) and put them in matching pairs.
Tuesday	Write a letter on each of several foam cups, making sure most are labeled with *K*. Stack the cups. A student selects the top cup and shows the letter to the group. If it features a *K*, another child pretends to pour tea into the cup with a toy or real kettle. Repeat with the other cups. ***Letter recognition***	Help each student make a simple kitten stick puppet. Point out that *kitten* starts with the /k/ sound. Then reread yesterday's story. Each time students hear the words *kitten* or *kittens*, they hold up their puppets and quietly say, "Meow."
Wednesday	Cut out a copy of the cards on page 69. Show a card to students. If the item on the card starts with *K*, students blow a kiss to you. If not, they sit still. ***Beginning sounds***	After reading *The Kissing Hand* by Audrey Penn, help each child trace his hand on a sheet of paper. On his tracing, the student glues a small cut-out heart labeled with *K*. Then he writes *K*s around his tracing, saying "*Kiss* starts with /k/" as he works.
Thursday	Staple the ends of a sentence strip together to make a crown. Also label index cards with letters, making sure most feature *K*. Have students stand, and select one child to wear the crown (king). The king shows a card to the group. If the card features a *K*, students bow to the king. If not, they stand still. Select a new king and repeat the activity. ***Letter recognition***	Use lipstick to make a lip print on each of several blank cards. Gather letter cards, including a set of *K* cards equal to the number of lip cards. After rereading yesterday's story, have students match each kiss card with a *K* card.
Friday	Show students a picture of a koala bear. Explain that *koala* starts with the /k/ sound. Then sing "Baby Koala" on page 67. Have children emphasize the /k/ sound in *koala* and act out the verb included in each verse. ***Beginning sounds***	To follow up *The Kissing Hand,* prepare one or more boxes of frozen french toast sticks. Remind students that Mrs. Raccoon told Chester her kiss would fill him with "toasty warm thoughts." Then have each child arrange three warm french toast sticks on his plate in the shape of a *K* before eating the treat.

Art and More!

Kaleidoscope Kite

(See the directions on page 68.)

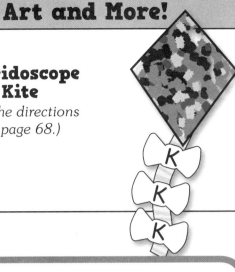

Practice Page: *See page 70 for letter-recognition and sound-association practice.*

Key Rubbings

(See the directions on page 68.)

Snack: When having a snack or lunch that involves ketchup, squirt each child's ketchup on his plate in a *K* shape. Have the child say, "/k/, /k/, ketchup!" before eating.

Class Book: For each child, make a large *K* with painter's tape on a sheet of art paper. A child paints over his picture with his favorite color of paint. When the paint dries, remove the tape. Bind the pages into a class book titled "Our *K* Kaleidoscope".

Songs and Such for the Week

Baby Koala
(Tune: "Did You Ever See a Lassie?")

Did you ever see a baby
Koala, koala?
Did you ever see it climbing
In the forest so green?

Did you ever see a baby
Koala, koala?
Did you ever see it walking
So slowly, so sweet?

Did you ever see a baby
Koala, koala?
Did you ever see it munching
On leaves big and green?

Did you ever see a baby
Koala, koala?
Did you ever see it sleeping
In a treetop so green?

We're Going to Learn About the Letter *K*
(Tune: "If You're Happy and You Know It")

We're going to learn about the letter *K*,
Yes, we're going to learn about the letter *K*.
Key, koala, kangaroo,
King and *kick* and *kitten* too.
Yes, we're going to learn about the letter *K*!

Art Activities

Kaleidoscope Kite

Tear colorful construction paper into small pieces. Spread glue inside part of a kite outline. Press the torn paper pieces on the glue. Continue until the entire kite is covered. Then cut out the kite. Tape a crepe paper streamer to the bottom of the kite as shown. Then glue cutout bows, each labeled with a *K*, to the streamer.

Key Rubbings

Use packing tape to tape several discarded keys onto a sheet of cardboard. A child places his paper atop the sheet of keys. After he removes the paper wrapping from a crayon, the child lightly rubs his paper with the side of the crayon until a key is revealed, saying "/k/, /k/, key" as he works. He repeats with other crayons until his paper is covered with key rubbings.

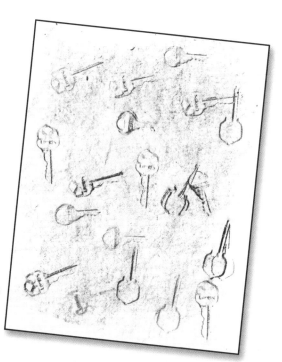

K Words

kale	kangaroo	Kansas	kayak	keep	ketchup
kettle	key	kick	kid	kind	king
kiss	kit	kite	kitten	kiwi	koala

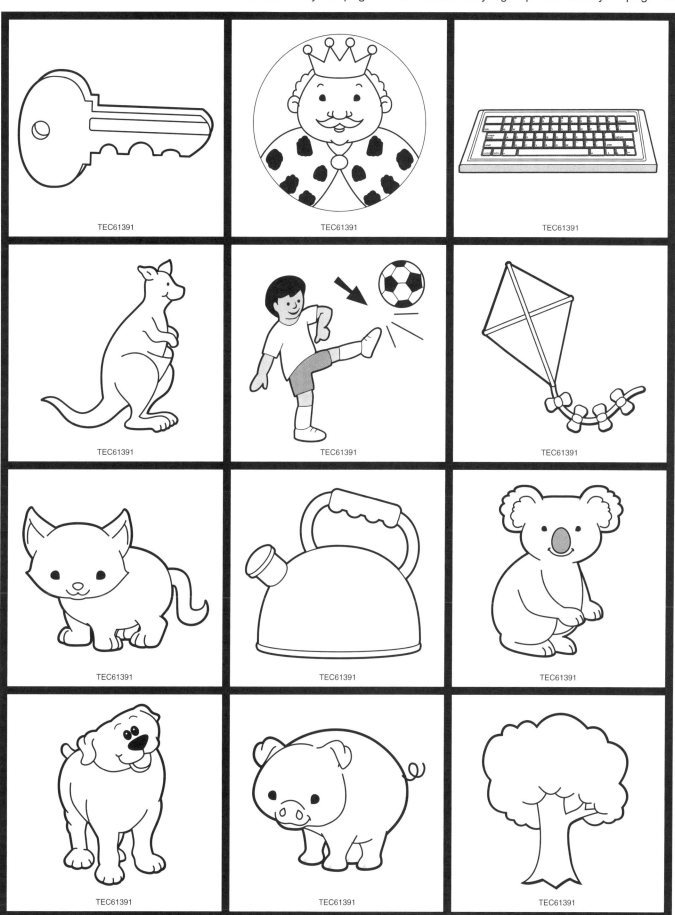

TEC61391

TEC61391

TEC61391

TEC61391

TEC61391

TEC61391

TEC61391

TEC61391

TEC61391

TEC61391

TEC61391

TEC61391

I Know About *K*!

Color the pictures that begin like 🦘.

Circle each **Kk**.

Kk

K	p	k	R
N	K	t	k
K	v	K	k

70   *Day-by-Day Alphabet Plans* • ©The Mailbox® Books • TEC61391

Centers for the Week

L Is for...

Lace: Place large *L* cards at a table along with glue and lengths of lace. A child chooses a card and puts glue on the letter. Then he presses lace into the glue. When the project is dry, he runs his hand over the letter and says its name.

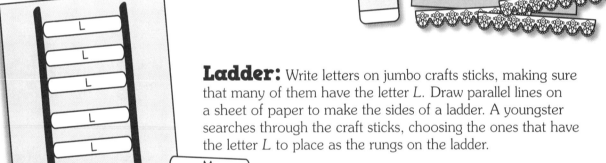

Ladder: Write letters on jumbo crafts sticks, making sure that many of them have the letter *L*. Draw parallel lines on a sheet of paper to make the sides of a ladder. A youngster searches through the craft sticks, choosing the ones that have the letter *L* to place as the rungs on the ladder.

Leaf: Provide several real or fake leaves, construction paper pages labeled with an outline of the letter *L*, and shallow pans of paint. A student chooses a page, drags a leaf through the paint, and then uses the leaf to trace the letter shape. She continues with other leaves and colors of paint.

	Group Time	Literature
Monday	Give a child an oversize *L* cutout and encourage him to stand in front of the class. Explain that he has the *L* because he is the leader. Then prompt the child to demonstrate a movement and encourage his classmates to follow the leader. Play several rounds of this game. ***Letter-sound connections***	Before reading the story *Llama Llama Red Pajama* by Anna Dewdney, write "llama" on your board and have students repeat the word, emphasizing the /l/ sound. Have students notice that *llama* begins with two Ls. Then show students pictures of llamas, prompting students to discuss observations about this animal.
Tuesday	Get a real or fake lemon and seat youngsters in a circle. Roll the lemon to a child and encourage her to say the /l/ sound. Then prompt her to continue the game by rolling it to another child. For an extra challenge, have each child name a word that begins with /l/. ***Reinforcing letter sounds***	Give each child a letter *L* card. During a second reading of the story *Llama Llama Red Pajama*, have each student hold up his card whenever he hears "llama, llama."
Wednesday	Place a length of yarn on the floor (line). Call on a student and guide him to name a word that begins with /l/. Next, encourage him to leap over the line and then take his seat. Continue with other youngsters. ***Beginning sounds***	Read aloud *Lunch* by Denise Fleming. After the story, give each child a large *L* cutout. Encourage each youngster to dip a paintbrush in paint and then flick it on the letter. Have her continue with other colors of paint so it resembles the mouse at the end of the story.
Thursday	Cut out a yellow copy of the lion face pattern on page 75. Label yellow construction paper strips with different letters, including several *L*s. Place the strips in a bag. Have a child draw a strip. If the strip has an *L*, have him place it next to the lion to begin a mane. Repeat the process until the lion has a full mane! ***Letter identification***	Make a supersize cutout of a lowercase *l*. Have each child look at the cover of *Lunch* and notice how it appears as if the mouse has been chewing on the letter *l*. Next, reread the story, encouraging youngsters to point out any *L*s on each page. For each *L*, help a child tear a small piece from the cutout, as if the mouse has chewed on it!
Friday	Make lollipop stick puppets and scatter them on the floor. Then arrange a variety of letter cards nearby, including an *L* for each lollipop. Lead students in reciting the rhyme "Lollipop!" on page 73. Then have each child locate a letter *L* card and place it over a lollipop. Play until all the lollipops have *L*s. ***Letter recognition***	What words begin with /l/? Remind students that *lunch* begins with /l/. Then help a student name another word that begins with /l/. Write the word on a sticky note and have the child attach the note to the book cover. Continue until the cover has several sticky notes.

Art and More!

Lovely Lobsters
(See the directions on page 74.)

L is for lobster.

Practice Page: *See page 76 for letter-recognition and sound-association practice.*

Peel an *L*
(See the directions on page 74.)

Gross Motor: Encourage little ones to line dance! Have students stand in a line. Prompt youngsters to isolate the beginning sound of the word *line.* Then play a recording of country music and encourage students to dance in any way desired.

Class Book: Have each child draw a picture of something that begins with an *L.* Copy her picture, reduced 50 percent. Then have the child cut out the reduced copy and attach it to the back of her original drawing. Label the pictures "Large [picture name]" and "Little [picture name]." Then bind the pages together to make a class book.

Large Ladybug

Songs and Such for the Week

Lollipop!
Lickety lick
The lollipop!
Lick at the bottom.
Lick at the top.
Lickety lick
The lollipop!
Lickety lick
And then you stop.

Limbo!
(tune: "Bingo")

There is a game that we can play,
And limbo is its name-o!
L-I-M-B-O!
L-I-M-B-O!
L-I-M-B-O!
And limbo is its name-o!

Art Activities

L is for lobster.

Lovely Lobsters

To make a lobster, paint the bottom of one foot red and make a print (lobster body) on a sheet of paper. Then make two handprints (claws) above the footprint. Dip a finger in red paint and use it to make lines from the claws to the body and to make eyestalks. Finally, attach eye cutouts to the eyestalks and write "L is for lobster" on the page.

Peel an *L*

This process art is easy to make and requires minimal supplies! To begin, attach masking tape to a sheet of paper to make a letter *L*. Use a foam brush to paint over the masking tape. Then, when the paint is dry, peel off the tape. Trace the letter and say its name!

Words

ladder	ladybug	lamp	leaf	leg
lemon	letter	light	lime	lion
lips	llama	lock	log	loop

TEC61391

I Know About L!

Color the pictures that begin like 🦁.

Circle each **Ll**.

Ll

H	D	L	c
l	h	l	L
l	L	F	L

Centers for the Week

M Is for...

Macaroni: Use a permanent marker to write the letter *M* on an unbreakable mirror. Then place the mirror at a table along with a container of macaroni. A child identifies the letter and then places macaroni on the letter.

Magazine: Provide magazines and plastic magnifying glasses. A child chooses a magazine and searches it for *M*s, using a magnifying glass as an aid. When he finds an *M*, he highlights it with a yellow marker or highlighter pen.

Magnets: Gather a large magnet and a smaller magnet. Attach a letter *M* cutout to a tray. Then suspend the tray between the seats of two chairs, securing it in place. A child places the small magnet on the letter and then moves the large magnet beneath the tray to trace the letter with the small magnet.

Group Time	Literature
Monday Use tape to make a large *M* on the floor. Play a musical recording and have students march around the area. Stop the music and prompt youngsters to quickly place one foot on the *M* and say, "Mmmm!" Continue for several rounds. ***Letter-sound association***	Read aloud *Mud* by Mary Lyn Ray. Discuss how *mud* begins with an *M*. Then have students fingerpaint with brown paint (mud) and encourage them to draw *M*s in the paint. 
Tuesday Draw letters on white square cutouts (marshmallows), making sure there are several *M*s. Place the marshmallows in a bag. Attach a large drawing of a mug to a wall. Have youngsters, in turn, choose marshmallows. If the marshmallow has an *M*, have him tape it to the mug. If it doesn't, have him place it aside. ***Letter identification***	Attach *M* cards to craft sticks (stick puppet). Then make a mound of brown play dough (mud). Have a child push a stick puppet in the mud and then name a word that begins with /m/. Continue in the same way with other youngsters.
Wednesday Place several mosquito cards (see page 81) on an *M* cutout. Say the /m/ sound and ask youngsters if they hear the sound. Tell them that the mosquitoes say /m/, and *mosquito* begins with *M*. Then have each child swat a mosquito card with a flyswatter, say the /m/ sound, and then remove the card from the letter. ***Letter-sound association***	Label muffin liners with letters, including several *M*s. Get a muffin tin. Read aloud *If You Give a Moose a Muffin* by Laura Numeroff. Afterward, have a child choose a liner and help him identify the letter. If it is an *M*, have him put the liner in the muffin tin. Continue with each remaining liner.
Thursday Crush mint leaves and place them in an opaque container with small holes in the lid. Seat students in a circle. Then play music while youngsters pass the mint. Stop the music and have the child with the mint sniff it and say, "Mmmm, mint!" Then have him name another word that begins with /m/. Play another round. ***Beginning sounds***	After a second reading of *If You Give a Moose a Muffin*, guide students in making muffins for snacktime. While students work, have them isolate the beginning sound in the word *muffin*.
Friday Draw a simple moon on chart paper. Help a child name a word that begins with /m/. Then encourage him to draw an *M* on the moon. Continue with other youngsters. ***Forming letters*** 	Open the book to the first page. Ask students to say, "Moose," and identify the first letter in the word. Have a child write an *M* on a sticky note and attach it to the moose on the page. Repeat the process whenever the moose shows up throughout the book.

Art and More!

Man in the Moon

(See the directions on page 80.)

Class Book:
Enlarge the hat pattern on page 81 and have each child cut out a copy. Have him glue his hat to a preprogrammed sheet of paper and then draw something that begins with *M* coming out of the hat. Have him dictate or write the object's name. Bind the pages into a book.

What's in the magic hat?

It's a monkey!

Minty Masterpiece

(See the directions on page 80.)

Practice Page: *See page 82 for letter-recognition practice.*

Gross Motor:
Draw a simple map of the school. Then draw a path on the map to get to a destination, such as the playground. Have students help follow the map to get to the destination. Then encourage students to play outside for several minutes.

Songs and Such for the Week

O Mosquito!

(tune: "O Christmas Tree")

O mosquito, O mosquito,
Your music is annoying!
O mosquito, O mosquito,
Your music is annoying!
You make a mmmm sound in my ear.
Mmmm, mmmm, mmmm, mmmm is
all I hear.
O mosquito, O mosquito,
Your music is annoying!

Marshmallows

Marshmallows, marshmallows in
your mug.
Put in some cocoa—glug, glug, glug!
Watch them melt; they look so fine.
Marshmallows, marshmallows, you're
all mine!

Man in the Moon

To make this simple project, use a permanent marker to draw a face on a circle of aluminum foil. Then brush diluted glue on the foil and press white tissue paper squares over the glue. Brush another layer of glue over the squares if needed. When the project is dry, trim the edges to remove excess tissue paper.

Minty Masterpiece

Add several drops of mint extract to red and white paint. Then use this scented medium to make stripes on large *M* cutouts. If desired, display the resulting masterpieces with the title "Mmmm, That's Minty!"

Words

macaroni	mail	man	map	mask
mat	mittens	monkey	moon	mop
motorcycle	mouse	mug	mule	mushroom

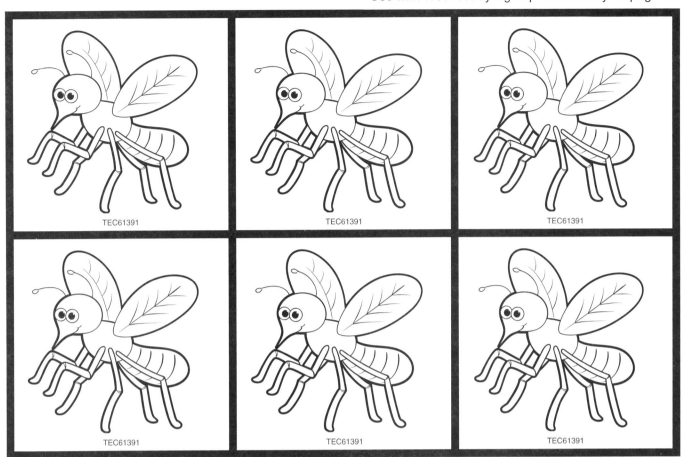

TEC61391 TEC61391 TEC61391

TEC61391 TEC61391 TEC61391

Magic Hat Pattern
Use with "Class Book" on page 79.

TEC61391

I Can Find M!

 Circle.

M   M   m

e   M   M   r

s   m   T   M

m   M

Centers
for the Week

N Is for...

Nest: Crumple a brown paper bag so it resembles a nest and gather a supply of plastic eggs. Use a permanent marker to label the eggs with a variety of letters, including several Ns. A child chooses an egg. If the letter is an N, he places it on the nest. If it is not, he attempts to identify the letter and then places it aside.

Newspaper: Attach newspaper to a tabletop and provide pens, pencils, crayons, and markers. Prompt a child to visit the center and draw Ns on the newspaper.

Night: For each child, use a white crayon to write a letter N on a sheet of black construction paper. A child traces the N with her finger and says, "N is for night!" Then she attaches star stickers to the letter.

	Group Time	Literature
Monday	Draw a large plate on a sheet of chart paper. Tell students that they are going to make a plate of nachos. Have youngsters say, "Nachos," emphasizing /n/. Then have a child draw an orange triangle chip on the plate and write an *N* on it. Continue with other youngsters until there is a full plate! ***Forming letters***	Help groups of three children arrange themselves on the floor to form the letter *N*. Then encourage students to pretend to take a quick nap. Next, prompt students to wake up and then read aloud *The Napping House* by Audrey Wood. 
Tuesday	Label a jar as shown and put slips of paper with students' names in the jar. Pull a name and then have students say nice things about the child. Repeat the activity throughout the day. ***Letter-sound association*** 	During a reread of *The Napping House,* call on youngsters to write the letter *N* on chart paper whenever the word *napping* is used in the story. Then have students count the *N*s.
Wednesday	Attach an *N* cutout to the floor. Then choose a student and say, "[Student name], be nimble. Jump and say a word that starts with *N* today!" Have the child jump over the letter and then say a word that begins with *N*. Continue with each child. ***Beginning sounds***	Read the story *Noisy Nora* by Rosemary Wells to your students. Then give each child a rhythm instrument. Say a word. If the word begins with /n/, have students make noise with their instruments. If it doesn't, have students stay silent. Continue with other words. 
Thursday	Place student name cards on the floor facedown. Have a child choose a card, flip it over, and encourage youngsters to identify the name. After pointing out the corresponding youngster, have her search for and point out any *N*s in her name. ***Letter recognition***	No doubt youngsters have experience making noise. Say, "Noisy [student name], how do you make noise?" Then prompt the child to name a way that she is noisy. Repeat the activity with different youngsters.
Friday	Recite "It's Nice to Have a Nose" on page 85. Prompt students to repeat the word *nose*, emphasizing /n/. Then have students share the names of things that are "nice" for noses (things they like to smell) and items that are "not nice" for noses (things they don't like to smell). ***Isolating beginning sounds***	Show youngsters the cover of the book. Have them point to the *N*s in the title. Have a student name (or invent) another name that begins with /n/ like *Nora*. Write the name on a sticky note and place it over *Nora*. Then read the new title aloud. Continue with other names that begin with /n/.

Art and More!

Noodle Collage
(See the directions on page 86.)

Practice Page: *See page 88 for letter-recognition practice.*

Nail-Pounding Project
(See the directions on page 86.)

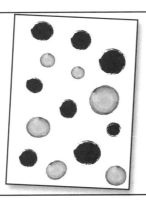

Snack: Show students a container of neapolitan ice cream. Have them locate the *N* in the ice cream name. Then encourage them to say, "Neapolitan," emphasizing /n/. Finally, give each child a small cup of neapolitan ice cream to try.

Class Book: What's in the nest? Give each child a copy of page 87. Encourage her to draw something in the nest. Then write her words to have her complete the sentence. Bind the book pages together with a cover titled "What is in the Nest?"

What is in the nest?

It is an elephant!

Sam

Songs and Such for the Week

Nibble!
Nibble, nibble, nibble,
Take a little bite.
Nibble, nibble, nibble,
Morning, noon, or night.
Nibble, nibble, nibble
On a noodle if you wish.
Nibble, nibble, nibble
On your very favorite dish!

It's Nice to Have a Nose
It's nice to have a nose
To smell a lovely rose,
To help you breathe or even sneeze.
A nose helps, I suppose!

N Art Activities n

Noodle Collage

To prepare, gather a variety of uncooked noodles and dye them different colors. Then glue the colorful noodles to a disposable plate. What lovely noodles!

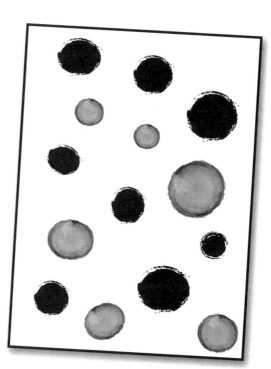

Nail-Pounding Project

Draw dots (nails) on a sheet of paper. Then place a dollop of paint on each nail and slide the paper into a large resealable plastic bag. Seal the bag and secure the opening with tape. Use a toy hammer to pound the nails. Then remove the sheet of paper to reveal a masterpiece!

N Words

nail	name	nap	necklace	needle
nest	net	newspaper	nickel	night
nine	nose	note	nurse	nut

What is in the nest?

It is

Note to the teacher: Use with "Class Book" on page 85.

I Can Find N!

 Circle.

N

b   n

N   V   n   U

H   n n   N   j

n   N   n

Centers
for the Week

ⓞ Is for...

Oatmeal: Partially fill a plastic container with oatmeal. Cut uppercase Os and lowercase o's from craft foam and hide them in the oatmeal. Provide two containers near the tub. Have students find the Os and sort them into the containers.

Octopus: Cut out a class supply of Os from construction paper. Provide shallow pans of paint and suction cups. Before youngsters visit the center, show them pictures of octopi and explain that octopi have suckers on their tentacles that are similar to suction cups. Then each youngster visits the center and makes suction cup prints on a letter O.

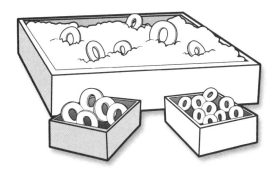

Octagon: Make a copy of page 93 for each child. Put the copies and a class supply of octagon cutouts at the center. A child colors and cuts out the cards. Then she glues cards with picture names that begin with the short O sound to the octagon.

	Group Time	Literature

Monday

Cut out a copy of the picture cards on page 93. For this activity, use only pictures whose names begin with a long *O* sound. Place the pictures on the floor and put a blue blanket over the cards to represent the ocean. Recite the first rhyme shown on page 91. Then have a child "dive" beneath the blanket to retrieve the appropriate card. Continue with the remaining cards. **Beginning sounds**

Read aloud *Officer Buckle and Gloria* by Peggy Rathmann. Give each child a star badge cutout and have him write "Officer [child's name]" on it. Have him notice that *Officer* begins with *O*. Then have him decorate his badge as desired.

Tuesday

Place letter cards, including eight *O*s, in a bag. Draw an octopus head on chart paper. Have a child draw a card and identify the letter. If it's an *O*, have her draw a tentacle on the octopus. Continue until the octopus has all eight tentacles. **Letter identification**

Have each child wear the badge he made on Monday and announce a safety tip to the class, such as "Officer Josh says to always wear your bike helmet!" Have the rest of the class say, "Okay, Officer Josh!" Repeat the activity with each youngster.

Wednesday

Say a word. If the word begins with the letter *O*, have each child make a large *O* with his arms. Repeat the activity with different words. **Beginning sounds**

Show youngsters the cover of *Ox-Cart Man* by Donald Hall. Have them find the letter *O* in the title of the story. Explain that the word *ox* begins with *O*. Ask youngsters what they think an ox is. What does an ox remind them of? What do they think an ox does? Then read the story aloud.

Thursday

Give each child a green olive slice and a black olive slice to taste. Label a chart as shown and have each child put a green *O*, a black *O*, or a red *O* (if she doesn't like olives) on the chart. **Beginning sounds**

black	O O O O O
green	O O
No, thank you	O O O

Transform a box so it resembles a cart. Cut out a copy of the cards on page 93 and place them in a bag. Then tell students that the man only wants to put things in his cart that have names that begin with short *O*. Have a child remove a card from the bag and name the picture. If the name begins with short *O*, have him place it in the cart. If it doesn't, have him put the card aside.

Friday

Cut an oval and an octagon from bulletin board paper and place them on your floor. Cut out a copy of the picture cards on page 93. Place the cards facedown. Have a child flip a card and say the picture name. If the name begins with a long *O* sound, have her sit on the oval. If it begins with a short *O* sound, have her sit on the octagon. **Differentiating between long- and short-vowel sounds**

Reread *Ox-Cart Man*, stopping on random pages to have students look for *O*s in the text. If an *O* is found, have a child write an *O* on a sticky note and attach it to the page.

Art and More!

Oval Art
(See the directions on page 92.)

Practice Page: *See page 94 for letter-recognition practice.*

Ollie Octopus
(See the directions on page 92.)

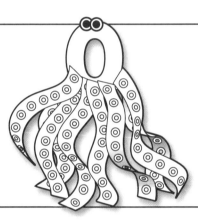

Snack: Set out a container with *O*-shaped cereal. Have each child place a large spoonful of the cereal in a resealable plastic bag. Then have her nibble on her little *O*s!

Class Book: Ask students to imagine what they will look like and do when they are old. Give each child a paper with the sentence starter shown. Then have her dictate (or write) to complete the sentence and draw a picture. Bind the finished pages together with a cover titled "When I Am Old."

When I am old... I will drive a really big car.

Songs and Such for the Week

In the Ocean
(tune: "Down in the Valley")

Down in the ocean,
The ocean so blue,
I think I see [overalls].
Tell me, do you?

Opposites

In and out,
Up and down,
Opposites are all around.
On and off,
Black and white,
Right and left,
Day and night.

Wiggly Octopus!
(tune: "If You're Happy and You Know It")

Oh, the octopus goes swimming in the sea.
He is wiggly and he's jiggly, you'll agree.
But if he gets quite a fright,
He will jet off out of sight,
And he'll leave some ink there where he used to be!

Art Activities

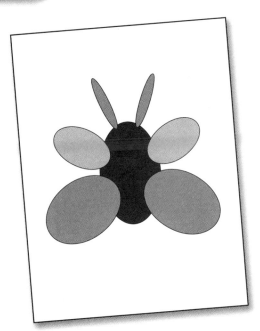

Oval Art

This abstract masterpiece has oodles of ovals! To prepare for this project, cut a variety of ovals. (Hint: Craft punches and die-cutting machines make this task a snap!) The student arranges the ovals on a sheet of paper as desired and glues them in place.

Ollie Octopus

Here's an adorable octopus craft just perfect for a unit on the letter O. To make one, attach eight construction paper strips (tentacles) to a letter O cutout (body). Glue eye cutouts to the body. Then press paper reinforcers on the tentacles so they resemble suckers. If desired, wrap the tentacles around a marker briefly to curl them. How cute!

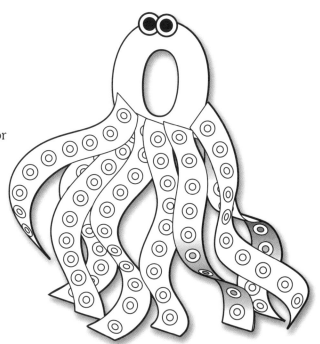

Words

oak	oatmeal	oboe	ocean	octagon	ogre
Ohio	Oklahoma	old	olive	open	opposite
ostrich	otter	out	oval	owl	ox

Picture Cards

Use with "Octagon" on page 89 and Monday's and Friday's group-time activities and Thursday's literature activity on page 90.

I Can Find O!

✏ Circle.

 o   P   O

o   W   O   D

e   O   G   o

O   o   X   O

    Day-by-Day Alphabet Plans • ©The Mailbox® Books • TEC61391

Centers
for the Week

P Is for...

Pillow: For this partner activity, provide several pillows and letter cards, including several cards with Ps. One youngster closes his eyes and the other child places a letter card beneath each pillow, making sure that some of them show Ps. The child opens his eyes and lifts a pillow. If there is a letter P beneath it, he says, "P is for pillow!" If there is a different card beneath the pillow, he says, "That's the wrong letter!" Then his partner replaces the card with one with the letter P. He continues with each remaining pillow, and then the youngsters switch roles.

Polka Dots: Provide colorful bingo daubers, hole-punch dots, and sticky dots as well as a class supply of pages with a large letter P. A child traces the letter with his finger and says, "/p/, /p/, /p/, polka dots." Then he uses the various items to decorate his P with polka dots.

Pizza: Decorate a circle of construction paper so it resembles a pizza without toppings. Draw a large letter P on the pizza and laminate it for durability. Then place it at a table along with play dough in a variety of colors. Students make toppings for the pizza and place them along the P. Then they run their hands over the toppings and identify the letter.

	Group Time	**Literature**
Monday	Cut out a copy of the penguin pattern on page 99 and place it in your classroom. Have youngsters scan the room for the penguin and then say "Peekaboo penguin!" when they see it. Call on a child to get the penguin and identify the letter on its tummy. To play another round, have students cover their eyes while you hide the penguin again. ***Letter identification***	Get a pad of colorful document flags. Read aloud *Pumpkin Pumpkin* by Jeanne Titherington. Then open the book to the first page and have a child find a letter *P* in the text. Have her flag the letter. Continue until several *P*s have been identified and flagged.
Tuesday	Put a supply of large pink and purple pom-poms in a container. Toss a pom-pom to a child and have her say, "[Color] pom-pom!" Help her name another word that begins with /p/ and then have her toss the pom-pom back in the container. Continue in the same way. ***Beginning sounds***	Place a pumpkin nearby. Reread the story *Pumpkin Pumpkin*. Then ask youngsters to recall events from the story. After a child shares an event, have him use a permanent marker to write a letter *P* on the pumpkin.
Wednesday	Gather letter cards, including several *P*s, and a bowl of pasta shapes. Have a child choose a card and show it to the class. Encourage youngsters to say whether the letter is a *P*. If it is, have the child say, "Pasta in the pot!" and place a spoonful of pasta in the pot. Continue with each card. ***Letter recognition***	Give each child a paper programmed with the letter *P*. Have her glue green yarn (pumpkin vine) to the letter. Then prompt her to attach leaf and pumpkin cutouts to the page. Have youngsters identify the letter and recall how Jamie watched the pumpkin grow.
Thursday	Get a potato and a source of upbeat music. Seat youngsters in a circle. Play the music as students quickly pass the potato. Stop the music and encourage the child with the potato to say a word that begins with /p/. Then restart the music. ***Beginning sounds*** 	Read aloud *If You Give a Pig a Pancake* by Laura Numeroff. Then toss a craft foam pancake to a child. Say, "If you give [student name] a pancake, [he] is going to want a…" Encourage the child to name something that begins with /p/ and toss the pancake back to you. Continue for several rounds.
Friday	Get a jar of pickles and a stack of small letter cards, including several *P*s. Place the cards in a bag. Recite the rhyme "Pickle Power!" on page 97. Then have students remove cards from the bag, attaching each letter P card to the pickle jar. Afterward, store the jar for safekeeping. ***Letter recognition***	In advance, make a pancake for each child. Prompt each child to squeeze syrup to "write" the letter *P* on his pancake. Prompt him to say, "/p/, /p/, pancake!" Then encourage him to eat his treat!

Art and More!

Paper Bag Pet
(See the directions on page 98.)

Practice Page: *See page 100 for letter recognition practice.*

Pom-Pom Press
(See the directions on page 98.)

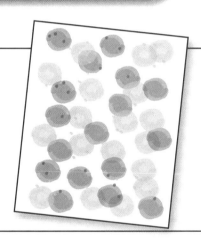

Snack: Have youngsters use butter knives to chop up canned peaches and pears. As they work, have them isolate the beginning sound /p/ in the words *peaches* and *pears*. Mix the chopped fruit in a bowl. Then serve this fruit salad for a snack!

Class Book: Help each child make a painting of something that begins with /p/. Label each painting similar to the one shown and have each child circle the *P*s in the sentence. Then bind the pages together with a cover titled "Perfectly Pleasing Paintings."

Evan painted pears.

Songs and Such for the Week

Pickle Power!
Pickles are green; pickles are sour;
I like to eat them any old hour!
I like their crunch.
I could munch a bunch!
Hooray for pickle power!

Puddle Stomping
(tune: "Did You Ever See a Lassie?")

Did you ever stomp a puddle, a puddle, a puddle?
Did you ever stomp a puddle on a wet, rainy day?
Did it splash and splatter
While rain pitter-pattered?
Did you ever stomp a puddle on a wet, rainy day?

P Art Activities

Pom-Pom Press

In advance, place large pom-poms next to pans of pink and purple paint. To make this masterpiece, press a pom-pom in a pan of paint. Then say, "/p/, /p/, /p/" as you make prints on the paper. Continue with the other color of paint until a desired effect is achieved.

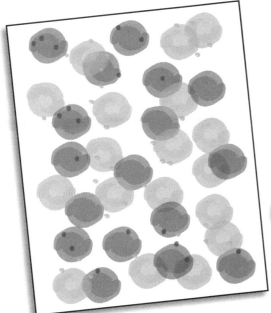

Paper Bag Pet

To make this adorable pet, cut ears and a nose from construction paper scraps and attach them to a lunch-size paper bag. Draw eyes and a mouth on the bag and add dots above the mouth. Decide on a name for the pooch that begins with the letter *P*. Write the name on a tag cutout. Then glue the tag to the bag and draw a collar.

P Words

pan	pants	pear	pencil	penguin
penny	person	piano	pie	pig
pillow	pizza	pocket	popcorn	pumpkin

TEC61391

I Can Find P!

 Circle.

P

u	D	p
G	p	P	c
P	M	p	V
P	p	F	p

Centers
for the Week

Q Is for...

Quick: Gather a stack of letter cards, including several Qs, and place the stack facedown. Two youngsters visit the center. One child flips the cards over quickly. His partner must be quick and snatch only the Qs as they are flipped over. When the stack runs out, the Qs are put back in the stack and the students switch roles.

Quarter: Gather cardboard or paper play money, including several quarters, and place it in a container. Draw a large Q on a sheet of paper. A child searches through the container, removing the quarters and placing them on the Q.

Queen: Gather the queen cards from two decks of cards as well as several number cards. Shuffle the cards and place the stack facedown. Two youngsters take turns flipping cards. Whenever a child flips a queen, she removes it from the stack. The first child with four queens is the winner of the round.

	Group Time	Literature
Monday	Make a class supply of uppercase and lowercase Q cards and hide the cards in your room. Then have students go on a quest for Qs. Encourage each child to find one uppercase and one lowercase card and bring them back to the group area. ***Uppercase and lowercase letters***	Cut out a copy of the picture cards on page 105. Read aloud *The Quilt Story* by Tony Johnston. Then place the pictures on the floor and have students identify each one. Put a quilt over the pictures. Slide your hand beneath the quilt and remove a picture. Then flip up the quilt and have students identify which picture is missing. Play several rounds.
Tuesday	Gather letter cards, including several Qs. Show youngsters a card. If the card shows a Q, have students quack loudly. If it shows another letter, have students identify the letter. Continue with each remaining card. ***Letter identification***	Gather youngsters around a quilt. Place letter manipulatives, including several Qs, in a container. Play music and have students pass the container. Stop the music and have the child with the container remove a letter. If it's a Q, she says its name and sound and then sits on the quilt until another child pulls a Q from the container.
Wednesday	Draw a large question mark on chart paper. Then say a random sentence to youngsters. If it's a question, have a child write a Q on the question mark. Repeat the activity with several different sentences. ***Writing letters***	Gather letter cards, including several Qs. Read aloud *The Very Quiet Cricket* by Eric Carle. Then have students chirp like crickets as you hold up the cards, one by one. Whenever you show them a Q card, they must be quiet. Any other letter is their cue to start again.
Thursday	Give each child a letter Q cutout. Explain that the word *quiet* begins with Q. Name a location, such as a library, a movie theater, or a basketball game. If this is a location where people should be quiet, have students raise their Qs and whisper "/kw/, /kw/, quiet!" If it's a location where people can be loud, have youngsters do nothing. Continue with several options. ***Beginning sounds***	Give each child a Q card. Reread *The Very Quiet Cricket*. Each time you read the text, "But nothing happened. Not a sound," have students hold up their Q cards and whisper, "Quiet, quiet, cricket!"
Friday	Cut squares of patterned scrapbooking paper to fit on a piece of poster board. Have a child use a marker to write Q on a square and then glue it to the board. When everyone has glued on a square, the result is a lovely Q quilt! ***Writing letters***	Give each child a paper labeled with a large Q. Have her attach a cutout copy of a cricket card on page 105 to the paper. Then encourage her to tell you about the story as you write her words in the middle of the Q.

Art and More!

Dot, Dot, Dot
(See the directions on page 104.)

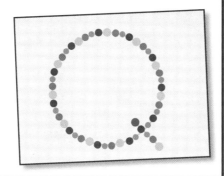

Practice Page: *See page 106 for letter-recognition practice.*

Mini Quilts
(See the directions on page 104.)

Transition: Call on a youngster and have him tiptoe quietly to his next activity. Continue with each remaining youngster, challenging each one to be even quieter than the last.

Class Book: Label a page with "Shhhh! It's quiet time." Have each child dictate (or write) words describing a time when she is quiet. Then have her draw a picture to illustrate her words. Bind the pages together with a cover labeled "Quiet Time."

Shhhh! It's quiet time. I am quiet when I listen to my mom read.

Songs and Such for the Week

Quack, Quack
(tune: "Mary Had a Little Lamb")

Hear the ducklings say, "Quack, quack,
Quack, quack, quack, quack, quack, quack."
Hear the ducklings say, "Quack, quack,"
And Mama quacks right back—*Quack!*

A Shiny Quarter
(tune: "We Wish You a Merry Christmas")

I have a new shiny quarter.
I have a new shiny quarter.
I have a new shiny quarter.
That's 25 cents!

Quiet
A [cloud] is quiet.
[Feathers] are too.
A [rabbit] is quiet.
Tell me—are you?

Repeat the poem, substituting students' ideas for the underlined words.

Art Activities

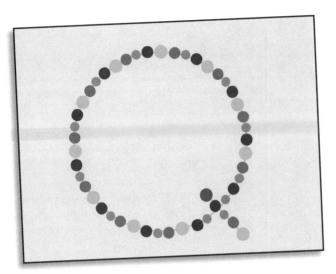

Dot, Dot, Dot
Gather a supply of Q-tip cotton swabs and prepare shallow pans of paint in several colors. To make a project, lightly draw a *Q* on a sheet of paper. Then dip a Q-tip into paint and make dots on the *Q*. Continue with other colors of paint, filling out the *Q*.

Mini Quilts
To make these miniature quilts, cut a variety of 2" x 2" fabric squares. Spread glue on a portion of an 8" x 8" sheet of paper and then press squares into the glue. Continue with more glue and squares until the piece of paper is covered and resembles a tiny quilt.

Words

quack	quail	quart	quarter	queen
quest	question	quick	quiet	quilt
quirk	quit	quite	quiz	quote

TEC61391

TEC61391

TEC61391

TEC61391

Cricket Cards

Use with Friday's literature activity.

TEC61391

TEC61391

I Can Find Q!

 Circle.

	P	q	b
q	Q	S	q
Q	D	q	Q
h	Q	w	q

Day-by-Day Alphabet Plans • ©The Mailbox® Books • TEC61391

Centers for the Week

R Is for...

Rubbing: Tape a tagboard *R* cutout to a tabletop. A child tapes a sheet of copy paper over the letter. Then she rubs the paper with the side of an unwrapped crayon. She continues with other crayons until a desired effect is achieved. For extra fun, provide *R* cutouts in corrugated cardboard, wallpaper, and Bubble Wrap cushioning material for different textures.

Road Race: Tape a strip of black paper (road) to a tabletop. Draw dashed lines down the center of the road and then divide the road into sections. Gather letter cards, including several *R*s, and stack the cards facedown. Provide toy cars. Two youngsters visit the center. One child draws a card and identifies the letter. If it's an *R*, he moves his toy car one space on the road. If the card shows another letter, his turn ends. Youngsters take turns until both cars reach the end of the road.

Roses: Make a copy of the gameboard on page 111 for each child. Obtain a cube-shaped box and label three sides with a lowercase *r* and three sides with an uppercase *R*. Two students each take a gameboard. One student writes an uppercase *R* on his first rose and the other child writes a lowercase *r* on hers. Students take turns rolling the die. Whenever the die matches a student's version of the letter, he writes his letter on a rose. The first player to label a dozen roses is the winner.

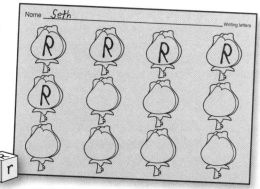

Group Time	Literature
Monday Give each child a letter *R* card and place a rug on the floor. Tell students that the *R* cards are their tickets to get on the rug. Have each child say the letter name and sound, give you the ticket, and then take a seat on the rug. Finally, have students help you count how many are on the rug! ***Reinforcing letter names***	Show youngsters the cover of *Rabbits & Raindrops* by Jim Arnosky. Ask students to look at the words in the title and ask them to share what they notice. Lead students to conclude that the words *rabbits* and *raindrops* both begin with *R* and the letter *R* makes the /r/ sound.
Tuesday Collect several medium-size rocks and hide them around the classroom. Write a large *R* on a piece of bulletin board paper and place it on the floor. Have students say, "Rock," leading them to notice /r/ at the beginning of the word. Then have students find the rocks and place them on the *R*. ***Beginning sounds***	Place raindrop die-cuts in a pocket chart. Hide a small picture of a rabbit behind one of the raindrops. Prompt a child to name a word that begins with /r/. Then encourage him to remove a raindrop to see if a rabbit is hiding behind it. Continue until the rabbit is found.
Wednesday Suspend a length of rope between two chairs. Write several words on separate cards, including many that begin with *R*. Choose a card and read the word aloud without showing it to your students. Have youngsters decide if the word begins with an *R*. If it does, prompt a child to use a clothespin to attach the card to the rope. ***Beginning sounds***	Show students *The Rainbow Fish* by Marcus Pfister. Ask, "Why do you think the fish is called 'Rainbow Fish'?" After students share, help them notice that *rainbow* begins with the letter *R*. See if they can find more *R*s on the cover of the book.
Thursday Draw letters on your board, including several *R*s. Use a pointer (or a dowel) to point to a letter. If you point to an *R*, encourage students to say the letter name and walk around the room like robots. If you point to a different letter, encourage students to identify the letter but stand still. ***Letter identification***	Draw a fish on chart paper. Provide aluminum foil scales and gather several letter cards, including many *R*s. Then hold up a card and encourage students to identify the letter. If it's an *R*, have a child use a glue stick to attach a foil scale to the fish. Continue with the remaining cards.
Friday Use markers to draw a rainbow on chart paper. Have each child, in turn, choose a marker color and write an uppercase *R* and lowercase *r* on the corresponding arc. ***Forming letters***	Display the two books. Encourage youngsters to notice that both book titles have the word *rain* in them. Give each child a raindrop die-cut and encourage her to place her raindrop on her favorite book. Then count and compare the sets of raindrops.

Art and More!

Rectangle Robot
(See the directions on page 110.)

Practice Page: *See page 112 for letter-recognition and sound-association practice.*

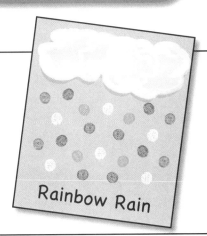

Rainbow Rain
(See the directions on page 110.)

Rainbow Rain

Snack: For snacktime, serve cut vegetables, such as cauliflower and thinly sliced carrot sticks. Have each child use a squeeze bottle of ranch dressing to make an *R* on her plate. Then encourage her to dip her veggies in the *R* and nibble on her snack.

Class Book: Have each child draw something that begins with /r/ on a sheet of paper. Write the object's name. Then encourage her to tape a rock cutout over the drawing to make a flap. Bind the finished pages behind a cover titled "What's Under the Rock?"

A ring!

Songs and Such for the Week

A Very Fine Color!
(tune: "For He's a Jolly Good Fellow")

Oh, red is a very fine color.
Red is a very fine color.
Red is a very fine color.
A [flower] can be red!

Repeat the song several times, inviting students to brainstorm substitutions for the underlined word.

Raindrops!

Raindrops, raindrops, all around,
In the sky and on the ground.
Raindrops, raindrops splash and splatter.
Pitter-patter, pitter-patter!

Red Rocket
(tune: "If You're Happy and You Know It")

Oh, I wish I had a rocket that was red.
Oh, I wish I had a rocket that was red.
I would fly around in space.
It's a fascinating place!
Oh, I wish I had a rocket that was red.

R Art Activities

Rectangle Robot
These robot crafts look terrific displayed in your classroom! To make a rectangle robot, cut a supply of gray rectangles. Then glue the rectangles to a colorful sheet of paper in a desired formation. Add details as desired.

Rainbow Rain
Pull apart cotton balls (clouds) and glue them to the top of a sheet of blue construction paper. Then dip some of your fingers in different colors of paint and "dance" your fingertips over the paper to make rainbow rain. When the paint is dry, label the paper "Rainbow Rain."

Rainbow Rain

R Words

rabbit	raccoon	radio	radish	rain	rainbow
rake	rat	ribbon	ring	road	robot
rock	rocket	rope	rose	round	rug

Name

Day-by-Day Alphabet Plans • ©The Mailbox® Books • TEC61391

Note to the teacher: Use with the third center activity on page 107.

I Know About R!

Color the pictures that begin like 🦝.

Circle each **Rr**.

Rr

R	r	p	R
W	R	r	B
R	Q	D	r

Centers
for the Week

S Is for...

Sand: Place letter manipulatives or cards in your sand table or sand tub, including several Ss. Provide shovels and sieves. A child uses the tools to search through the sand and find the Ss. Then he places them in a separate container.

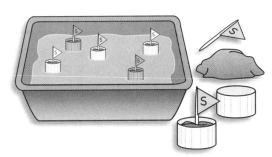

Sailboat: In advance, write Ss on separate construction paper triangles and tape them to toothpicks. Place the resulting sails in the center along with play dough, bottle caps, and a tub of water. A child pushes some play dough into a bottle cap and then sticks a sail in the dough to make a tiny sailboat. He says, "Sailboat," emphasizing /s/. Then he places his sailboat in the water.

Seal: Cut out eight copies of the seal pattern on page 117. Also make several circle cutouts (balls). Label eight balls with the letter S and the remaining balls with other letters. Place the balls facedown. Two students visit the center. One child flips a ball and identifies the letter. If it's an S, he places the ball above a seal's nose. If it isn't, he sets it aside. His partner repeats the process. Youngsters continue until all the seals have balls to balance.

Group Time	Literature

Monday

Get a suitcase. Hide *S* cards around the room. Have students say, "Suitcase," emphasizing /s/. Explain that *suitcase* begins with *S.* Then have youngsters hunt for the *S*s and place them in the suitcase. ***Reinforcing letter names***

Show youngsters the cover of the book *The Giant Jam Sandwich* by John Vernon Lord and have them locate the *S* in the title. Then prompt each child to name his favorite type of sandwich. After each child has a chance to share, read the story aloud.

Tuesday

Gather a stack of letter cards, including several *S*s. Hold up a card and have students identify the letter. If it's an *S,* prompt them to give it the "seal of approval" by clapping their hands as if they were flippers and making seal noises. Continue with the remaining cards. ***Letter identification***

Have students make a giant *S* sandwich! Place a supersize bread slice cutout at a table and have students spread red paint (jam) over the bread slice. Then have each child press an *S* card into the jam before placing an identical bread slice cutout on top.

Wednesday

Place letter cards in a container, including several *S*s. Have youngsters sit in a circle. Then encourage them to pass the container around the circle. Say, "Stop," and prompt the child with the container to pull out a letter card. If the card shows an *S,* have students say "/s/." If not, have them stay silent. Continue for several rounds. ***Letter recognition***

Have students look at the cover of *Silly Sally* by Audrey Wood. Direct them to notice that both of the words begin with *S.* Next, say, "Silly [student name]," modifying the name so that it begins with /s/. For example, say, "Silly Sack" instead of "Silly Jack." Continue with other students. Then read the story aloud.

Thursday

Make a yellow circle cutout (sun) and yellow strips (rays). Have a child name a word that begins with /s/ and then place a ray on the sun. Continue until each child has a turn to add a ray. ***Beginning sounds***

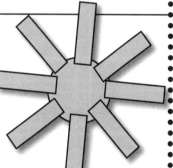

Have students say the word *silly,* prompting them to notice that the word begins with /s/. Ask students to name things they saw in the book that were silly. Then encourage them to name things they do that are silly!

Friday

Place a construction paper bread slice on the floor. Then ask, "What shall we add to our sandwich?" Encourage a child to name something that begins with *S.* Write the word on a strip of paper and have him place it on the bread. Continue with other youngsters, adding to the silly sandwich. Then place a final bread slice cutout on top! ***Beginning sounds***

Have each child write or dictate to tell which book was his favorite. Then encourage him to circle any *S*s in the writing and draw a picture to illustrate his words.

Art and More!

Sea and Sun
(See the directions on page 116.)

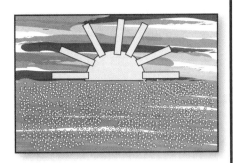

Practice Page: *See page 118 for letter-recognition practice.*

A Sandy *S*
(See the directions on page 116.)

Snack: Have youngsters make saltine sandwiches! Give each child cheese slices and pairs of saltine crackers. Youngsters sandwich the cheese slices between saltine crackers to make little sandwiches. Yum!

Class Book: Give each child a sheet of paper programmed with the words "*S* Is Super!" Then instruct her to think of something that begins with the letter *S*. Encourage her to draw a picture on the paper and then write or dictate the object's name. Bind the pages together with a cover labeled "*S* Is Super!"

S Is Super!

sandwich

Songs and Such for the Week

Make an *S*
(tune: "Are You Sleeping?")

First, curve this way.
Then curve that way.
Make an S.
Make an S.
Sack and *seal* and *sandwich,*
Soup and *sun* and *seven*
Start with S,
Start with S.

Soap!
(tune: "Clementine")

Soap is slippery, soap is sudsy,
Soap is special—yes, it's true.
Soap will get germs off your body.
Soap is great for me and you!

S Art Activities

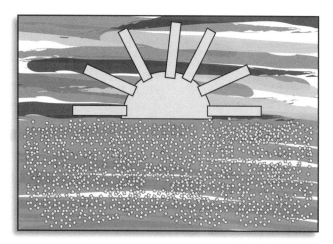

Sea and Sun

To make this serene sunset, brush blue paint (sea) along the bottom half of a sheet of paper. Sprinkle silver glitter over the paint. Then brush stripes of orange, red, and yellow paint above the blue paint so it resembles a sunset. Finally, glue a yellow semicircle cutout and strips (sun and sun rays) above the blue paint. How lovely!

A Sandy *S*

This sandy process art is simple to make! Make a page labeled with a letter *S* as shown. Then brush glue over a portion of the letter and sprinkle colored sand over the glue. Continue brushing glue and sprinkling sand until the entire letter is covered. Then shake off the excess sand.

S Words

sad	sail	salt	sandwich	saw	scissors
seashell	sell	serve	seven	sigh	sing
sink	sit	six	soap	sound	sun

TEC61391

TEC61391

I Can Find S!

 Circle.

S			
r	f		S
S	B	s	z
s	S	M	S
h	s	E	S

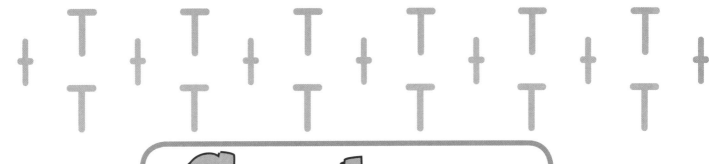

Centers
for the Week

T Is for...

Teeth: Cut white craft foam into small squares (teeth). Label some teeth with *T*s and the remaining teeth with other letters and place them in a container. Provide tongs and a simple mouth drawing as shown. A youngster uses his tongs to remove only teeth that have *T*s, placing them on the mouth. He continues until the mouth is full of teeth.

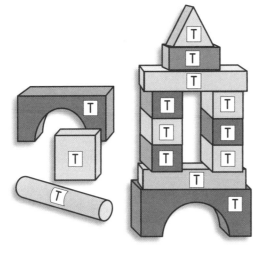

Tower: Attach *T* cards to building blocks. A youngster uses the blocks to build a tower. Then he counts the number of *T*s in his tower before he topples his construction!

Tea: Provide plastic tea cups and saucers, a tablecloth, and paper scraps. Youngsters set up for a tea party and then write *T*s on paper scraps and place them in the cups. What a tasty cup of *T*!

Group Time	Literature

Monday

Place four teddy cutouts (see page 123) in your pocket chart. Have students cover their eyes as you place a *T* card behind a teddy. Then prompt students to open their eyes. Say, "Tap a teddy!" and have a child choose a teddy and tap it two times. Lift the teddy to check. If there isn't a *T*, continue until the *T* is found. If there is a *T*, rehide the *T* for another round. ***Beginning sounds***

Attach apple die-cuts to ten small blocks. Read aloud *Ten Apples Up on Top* by Theo. LeSieg. Each time an apple is placed on top, have a student stack a block. At the end, have a child place a long block on top of the tower of apples so it resembles a letter *T*. Have students notice that *Ten* and *Top* both begin with *T*.

Tuesday

Cut out several copies of the tulip pattern on page 123. Place letter cards on the floor, including several *T*s. A child takes a tulip pattern and tiptoes through the cards, looking for *T*s. When he finds a *T*, he places his tulip on the card. Continue until all the *T* cards have tulips. ***Letter recognition***

Youngsters make other sets of ten with this activity. Gather a variety of manipulatives and write "ten" on separate index cards. Have a child count out ten manipulatives and then place a "ten" card on the pile. Encourage her to say, "Ten," and emphasize /t/ at the beginning of the word. Continue with other manipulatives.

Wednesday

Pair students; then play a musical recording and have students dance. Stop the music, encouraging students to quickly find their partners and then lie on the floor to make a *T* shape with their bodies. Continue for several rounds. ***Forming letters, reinforcing letter names***

Read aloud *Tooth Fairy* by Audrey Wood. Write "tooth" on a slip of paper. Have students notice that "tooth" begins with *T*. Ask a child to name another word that begins with *T*. Write that word on a slip of paper and have the child place that slip beneath a pillow. Continue with other words.

Thursday

Write a variety of letters, including several *T*s, on the board. Have each child decorate a small cardboard tube with *T*s. Have a child hold his *T* tube up to one eye and spot a *T* on the board. Have him circle the *T*. Continue with other youngsters until all the *T*s are circled. ***Letter recognition***

Have a child use a small square block and white paint to make prints on a sheet of paper so it resembles the Tooth Fairy's palace. Then have her drizzle glue on the paper in the shape of a *T* and shake glitter over the *T*. *T* is for *tooth*!

Friday

Get two toy telephones and give one to a child. Pretend to call her and then say, "Hello, [child's name]! Can you tell me a word that begins with /t/?" Help her name a word that begins with /t/. Then repeat the activity with another child. ***Beginning sounds***

Attach an apple cutout and a tooth cutout to separate craft sticks to make pointers. A child chooses a pointer and the corresponding book. Then she opens the book and points to a letter *T* in the text. Repeat the activity several times.

Art and More!

Tape a *T*
(See the directions on page 122.)

Practice Page: *See page 124 for letter-recognition and sound-association practice.*

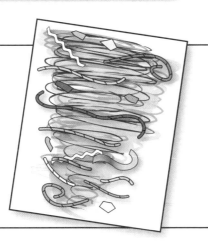

Terrific Tornadoes!
(See the directions on page 122.)

Transition: Gather student name cards. Show a card and have students identify the name and locate any *T*s that might be in the name. Then have the child tiptoe to the next activity.

Class Book: Label a paper "Talk, Talk, Talk! Who do you like to talk to?" and make a copy for each child. Encourage a child to locate the *T*s on the page, dictate to answer the question, and then draw a picture. Bind the finished pages together with the title "Talk, Talk, Talk!"

Talk! Talk! Talk!
Who do you like to talk to?

I like to talk to *my* little sister. She is *just* a baby, and she can't talk back to me yet.

Songs and Such for the Week

Tiptoe Past the Tiger
Tiptoe, tiptoe past the tiger.
It is toothy, scary too!
If you tiptoe oh so softly,
Maybe it will not see you!

Toast Toppings
(tune: "Twinkle, Twinkle, Little Star")

What do you like on your toast?
Tell me what you like the most.
Do you top it with some jam,
Tuna, cheese, or maybe ham?
What do you like on your toast?
Tell me what you like the most.

Art Activities

Tape a *T*

This simple artwork reinforces the shape of this letter *T*! To make this masterpiece, attach masking tape to fingerpaint paper to make *T*s. Then fingerpaint over the surface of the paper, using desired colors. When the paint is dry, remove the tape to reveal the *T*s. Neat!

Terrific Tornadoes!

This colorful tornado looks lovely on display in a classroom. Gather a variety of arts-and-crafts supplies, such as crayons, markers, paint, yarn, ribbon, and paper strips. Use crayons and markers to draw a swirling tornado on a sheet of paper. Next, use paint to add to the tornado. Then glue yarn, ribbon pieces, and paper strips as desired. What a terrific tornado!

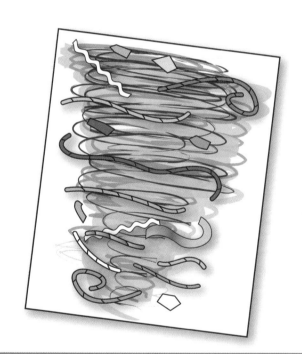

T Words

table	taco	tail	tank	tape	telephone
ten	tent	tie	tire	toast	tomato
tooth	tornado	towel	toy	turkey	turtle

Teddy Bear Pattern
Use with Monday's group-time activity on page 120.

TEC61391

Tulip Pattern
Use with Tuesday's group-time activity on page 120.

TEC61391

I Know About *T*!

Color the pictures that begin like 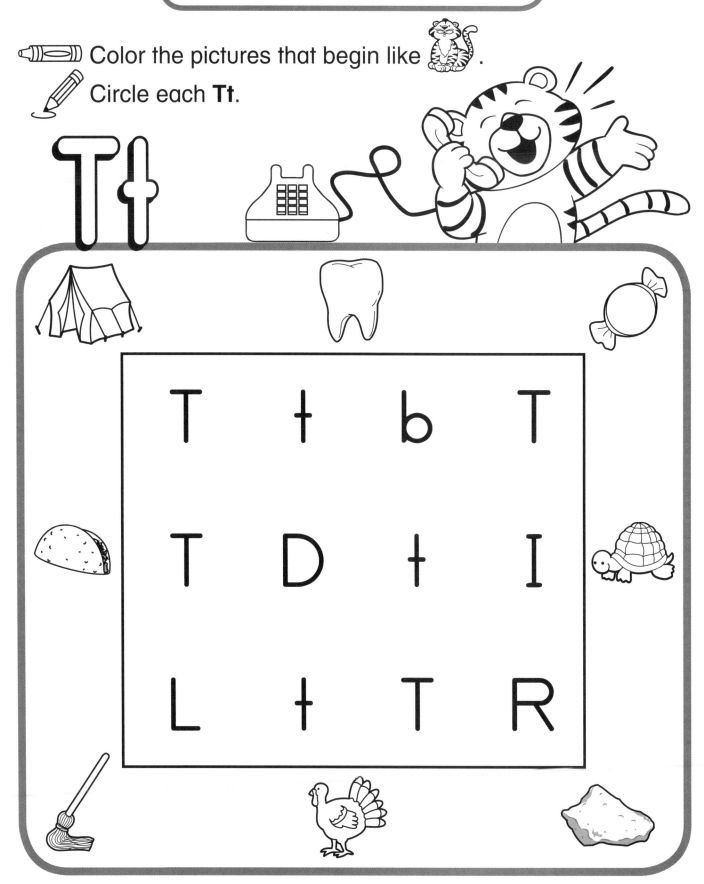.

Circle each **Tt**.

T	t	b	T
T	D	t	I
L	t	T	R

Centers for the Week

U Is for...

Unicorn: Enlarge the unicorn pattern on page 129 and then make a class supply. Cut paper reinforcers in half (keep the reinforcers on the backing paper) so they resemble the letter *U* and place them at a center. A child colors a unicorn and then attaches little *U*s all over the magical creature!

Underline: Place magazines and newspapers at a table along with colorful markers. Youngsters look through the periodicals and underline any *U*s they see.

Under: Cut out a copy of the cards on page 129 and place them at a center along with a large opaque cup. Two youngsters visit the center. One child studies the cards and then closes his eyes. His partner puts one of the cards under the upside-down cup. Then the youngster opens his eyes and identifies the missing card by saying, "The [umbrella] card is under the cup!" Students switch roles and play the game again.

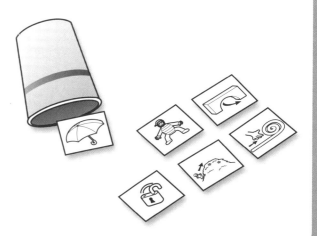

	Group Time	Literature

Monday

Cut out copies of the unicorn pattern on page 129. Arrange letter cards on your floor, making sure that several of them are *U*s. Call on a child and give him a unicorn. Instruct him to place the unicorn on a *U*. Repeat the activity until all the *U*s are covered. *Letter recognition*

Read aloud *Underwear!* by Mary Elise Monsell. Then give each child a simple underwear cutout similar to the ones worn in the story. Encourage her to write *U* on the underwear. Then have her decorate it as desired.

Tuesday

Hide *U* cutouts or cards around your room and place an upside-down umbrella on the floor. Have youngsters search for the letters. When they find one, they say the short *U* sound and then place the letter in the umbrella. *Letter sounds*

Write letters on chart paper, including several *U*s. Have a child find a *U*, circle it, and then try to say, "*U* is for *underwear!*" without laughing. Hopefully he will have more luck than the buffalo in the story! Continue until all the *U*s are circled.

Wednesday

Place letter cards in a bag, including several *U*s. Play music and encourage youngsters to pass the bag around the circle. Stop the music and have a child take a card. If the card is a *U*, have him sit in the middle of the circle and hold an open umbrella. Continue the game, having the next child who draws a *U* take his place. *Letter recognition*

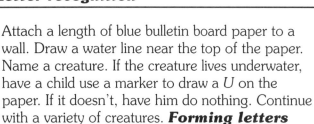

Read aloud *The Umbrella* by Jan Brett. Have each child make a simple umbrella craft. Then encourage him to dictate what happens in the story. Turn the umbrella upside down and then write his words on the craft.

Thursday

Attach a length of blue bulletin board paper to a wall. Draw a water line near the top of the paper. Name a creature. If the creature lives underwater, have a child use a marker to draw a *U* on the paper. If it doesn't, have him do nothing. Continue with a variety of creatures. *Forming letters*

Give each child a *U* card. Reread the story, having students hold up their letter cards whenever they hear the word *umbrella*.

Friday

Arrange students so they have space to move. Say a word. If the word begins with /ŭ/ (or /ū/ if you are working on the long-vowel sound), instruct students to curl up on the floor, making a *U* shape with their bodies. Play several rounds of this activity. *Beginning sounds*

Display *Underwear!* and *The Umbrella*. Give each child a *U* card and have him place it on his favorite book. Then help students count and compare the number of *U*s, using the words *less, more,* and *equal*.

Art and More!

A Handy Umbrella

(See the directions on page 128.)

Practice Page: *See page 130 for letter-recognition practice.*

A Magical *U*

(See the directions on page 128.)

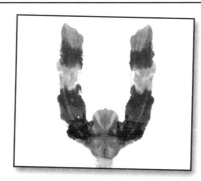

Snack: Have little ones mix up a tasty mess-free snack, such as an assortment of cereal in a resealable plastic bag. Then encourage each child to eat his snack while sitting under a table! What a fun way to spotlight *U*.

Class Book: Give each child a page labeled "Uh-oh!" Have her locate the *U*. Then have her draw a picture about a time when she had an "uh-oh" situation, such as breaking something, falling, or knocking something over. Write her description of her experience beneath the picture. Then bind the pages together to make a class book.

Uh-oh!

I broke my mom's vase!
—Anna

Songs and Such for the Week

Upside Down

(tune: "Three Blind Mice")

Upside down,
Upside down,
See how it looks
While turned around.
It's really fun to be upside down.
The ground is the sky, and the sky is the ground.
I think that it is the best thing around
To be upside down.

Only One Horn

(tune: "The Farmer in the Dell")

A unicorn has one horn.
A unicorn has one horn.
It's that way when it's born.
A unicorn has one horn.

Art Activities

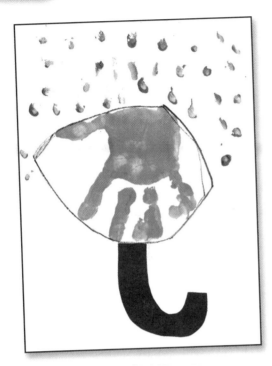

A "Hand-y" Umbrella

To make this adorable umbrella, press a hand into a shallow pan of paint and then make a print with fingers spread on a sheet of colorful construction paper. Draw an outline around the print so it resembles an umbrella. Then add a construction paper handle to the project. Dip a cotton swab in blue paint and then make prints (raindrops) on the page.

A Magical *U*

Here's a simple piece of process art that results in a lovely letter masterpiece! To make one, fold a sheet of construction paper in half. Then open the paper. Use a paintbrush and different colors of paint to make half of a letter *U* on one half of the paper. Fold the paper, smooth it with your hand, and say some magic words. Then open the paper to reveal the letter *U*!

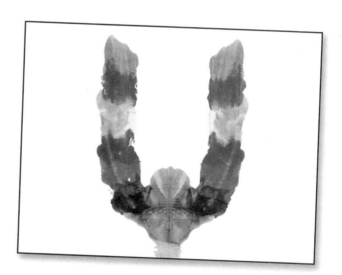

U Words

ugly	ukulele	umbrella	uncle	under
underwater	underwear	unhappy	unicorn	unicycle
uniform	unusual	up	use	utensils

Unicorn Pattern

Use with "Unicorn" on page 125 and Monday's group-time activity on page 126.

TEC61391

Picture Cards

Use with "Under" on page 125.

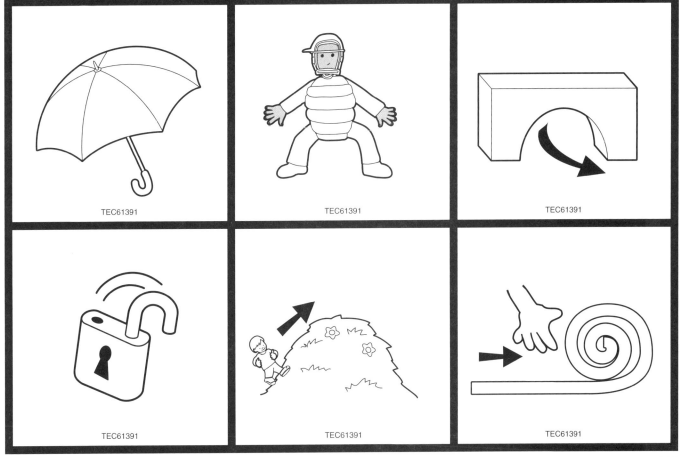

I Can Find *U*!

 Circle.

U

V   u

u   U   W   u

X   u   U   C

U   u   F   U

Day-by-Day Alphabet Plans • ©The Mailbox® Books • TEC61391

Centers
for the Week

 Is for...

Volcano: Place red paper (lava) on the floor and scatter several letter manipulatives on the paper, including several Vs. Youngsters have to quickly grab the Vs from the volcano lava. Then they dump the Vs back into the mix and play the game again!

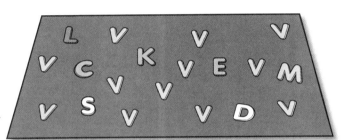

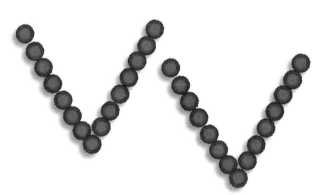

Violet: Provide purple pom-poms (violets). A child arranges violets on the floor to form Vs.

Vine: Cut out several copies of the leaf pattern on page 135. Label each leaf with a letter, including several Vs. Place a length of green yarn on the floor. A child finds the leaves that have Vs and places them next to the yarn to make a vine.

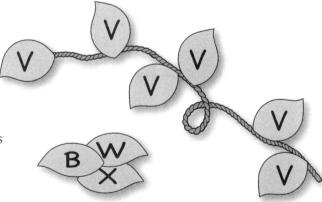

	Group Time	Literature
Monday	Show youngsters a picture of a violin. Write *violin* on your board. Have students say the word, drawing out the /v/ sound. Listen to a recording of violin music. Periodically stop the music and have students say, "/v/, /v/, violin!" ***Beginning sounds*** 	Attach a *V* card to a soup ladle. Read aloud *Growing Vegetable Soup* by Lois Ehlert. Have students sit in a circle and pass the ladle. On occasion, say, "Stop" and have the child with a ladle say, "/v/, vegetable" and then name a vegetable she would put in soup. Play several rounds.
Tuesday	Wear a vest. Gather a variety of letter cards, including several *V*s, and place them in a bag. Have a child choose a card. If the card has a *V* on it, help him tape the card to your vest. Continue with each remaining card. ***Letter recognition***	Give each child a large letter *V* cutout. Have her press cut vegetables in a shallow pan of paint and then make prints on the *V*.
Wednesday	Say a word. If the word begins with /v/, have students pretend to vacuum the floor. If the word does not begin with /v/, have students stand still. Play several rounds of this fun activity! ***Beginning sounds***	Gather a suitcase and several items to pack. Read aloud *Arthur's Family Vacation* by Marc Brown. Tell students that you think everything you pack for your vacation should begin with /v/. Pick up a shirt and say, "First, I'll pack my 'virt'!" Youngsters are sure to giggle! Continue with other items, changing their names so they begin with /v/.
Thursday	Cut out the violet pattern on page 135 and attach it to a jumbo craft stick or an unsharpened pencil to make a pointer. Write several letters, including many *V*s, on the board. A child uses the violet pointer to point to a *V*. Write his name next to the *V* he located. Then continue with other youngsters. ***Letter recognition***	Write "Vacation" on chart paper. Have students say the word, emphasizing /v/. Then ask students to name things that Arthur does on his vacation. Write their ideas beneath the heading.
Friday	Draw a volcano on chart paper. Name a word. If the word begins with /v/, have a child draw a red *V* on the volcano. Repeat the activity several times until the volcano is covered with *V*s. ***Writing letters***	Gather *V* cutouts. Ask a child to talk about a time she went on vacation. After she is done sharing, have her attach a *V* to a sheet of chart paper. Continue with each remaining student.

Art and More!

Down in the Valley
(See the directions on page 134.)

Practice Page: *See page 136 for letter-recognition and sound-association practice.*

Vibrant *V*
(See the directions on page 134.)

Snack: Cut vegetables into thin slices and provide ranch dip. A child takes several veggie slices and some dip. Then he forms *V*s with his veggies before eating them!

Class Book: Have each child draw a picture of the best vacation he has been on or would like to go on. Encourage each child to dictate information about the drawing. Write his words below his picture. Then bind the pages together and title the book "My Very Best Vacation."

I went to the beach and played a lot. The sand was hot!

Songs and Such for the Week

V Says /v/!
(tune: "Twinkle, Twinkle, Little Star")

V says /v/ in *vest* and *vine*,
Vacuum too and *valentine*,
Vegetables and *violin*—
Now let's all say /v/ again.
V says /v/ in *vest* and *vine*,
Vacuum too and *valentine*.

Make a *V*
(tune: "Row, Row, Row Your Boat")

Make, make, make a *V*
With your fingers now!
Make a *V*; make a *V*.
Let me show you how.

Art Activities

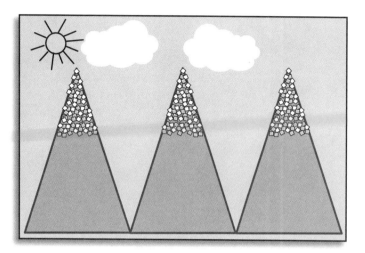

Down in the Valley

To make this project, cut triangles from a construction paper strip and attach them to a sheet of construction paper to make mountains. Spread glue on the top of each mountain, sprinkle white glitter on the glue, and add any other desired details. Notice that between each mountain is a valley and each valley is shaped like the letter *V*.

Vibrant *V*

Paint a sheet of paper so it is covered with vibrant colors. Then cut a letter *V* from black construction paper. (Hint: Folding the paper in half makes cutting the letter a simple task!) Set the cutout aside for another project. Then place the remaining black paper over the original painting. What a lovely, vibrant *V*!

V Words

vacation	vacuum	valley	van	vanilla	vapor
vase	vat	vegetable	veil	velvet	vent
very	vibrant	violet	violin	volcano	volume

Leaf Pattern
Use with "Vine" on page 131.

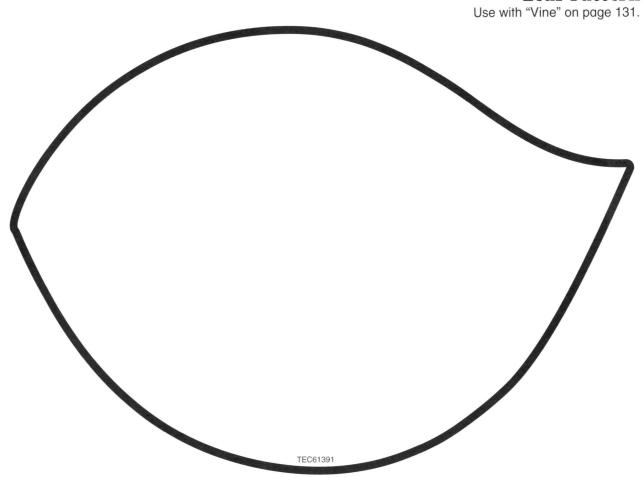

TEC61391

Violet Pattern
Use with Thursday's group-time activity on page 132.

TEC61391

I Know About V!

Color the pictures that begin like 🎻.

Circle each **Vv**.

V v

V	v	W	V
M	V	v	L
V	v	H	V

Centers
for the Week

W Is for...

Water: Fill your water table and place plastic letter manipulatives in the water, including several Ws. (Letters die-cut from craft foam also work well for this activity.) Provide a net. A child attempts to scoop only the Ws from the water.

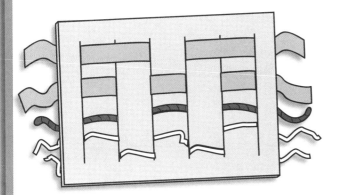

Weaving: Cut slits in sheets of craft foam and place it at a table along with ribbon, yarn, raffia, and other weaving materials. A student chooses a material and weaves it through the slits in the foam as desired. As he works, he says, "/w/, /w/, weave!" He continues with other materials as desired.

Worms: Place uncooked oatmeal in a tub and then place pieces of brown yarn (worms) in the tub. Provide large W cards. A child searches through the oatmeal and discovers a worm. Then she places the worm on the W. She continues with other worms until the letter is covered. Then she begins a new card!

Group Time	Literature

Monday

Write a large *W* on chart paper. Have several volunteers trace the letter with colorful markers. Encourage students to notice how the volunteers' arms move down, up, down, and up to write the letter. Prompt students to stand and then to crouch, stand, crouch, and stand again to mimic this movement. ***Writing letters***

Show students the cover of *Where the Wild Things Are* by Maurice Sendak. Have youngsters notice that *wild* begins with the letter *W*. Write "What is *wild*?" on your board. Have students explain what they think *wild* is. Write their ideas beneath the question. Then read the story aloud.

Tuesday

Write the following words on the board: *wave, wiggle, waggle, waddle.* Have students say the words, listening for the /w/ sound. Then have youngsters circle the *W* in each word. Next, have students practice a movement for each word. Randomly call out a word and have a child perform that movement. Continue in the same way. ***Beginning sounds, letter recognition***

Have each student fashion his own wild thing. Provide a variety of craft supplies and encourage each child to create a wild thing on a sheet of construction paper. Then have him glue die-cut *W*s around his creation. *W* is for *wild!*

Wednesday

Teach students how to wink. Have them say, "Wink," noticing that the word begins with /w/. Next, say a word. If the word begins with /w/, instruct each child to give her best wink. Repeat the activity with other words. ***Beginning sounds***

Gather students in a circle and then place a watermelon in the middle. Scatter letter cards around it, including several *W*s. Have youngsters find the *W*s and attach them to the watermelon. Then read aloud *Watermelon Day* by Kathi Appelt.

Thursday

Say, "*Wish* begins with *W*." Give each child a *W* card or cutout. Then call on a child and ask, "What would you wish?" Have the child name something he would wish for. Then have him hand you his *W* card. Continue with each remaining child. ***Reinforcing letters, beginning sounds***

Program a paper with "My watermelon is as cold as…" and make a copy for each child. Remind her how cold Jesse's watermelon is. Then help her dictate words to describe something very cold. Have her illustrate her sentence.

Friday

Place letter cutouts or cards in a gift bag. Have a child choose a letter. If she chooses a *W*, direct her to tape the letter to a wall. Play this game until all the letters have been removed from the bag. ***Letter recognition***

Have students sit in a circle. Roll a small watermelon to a child and have her say a word that begins with /w/, with help as needed. Encourage her to roll the watermelon to a classmate to continue the game.

Art and More!

Wonderful Watermelon
(See the directions on page 140.)

Practice Pages: *See pages 141 and 142 for letter-recognition and sound-association practice.*

Patterned Wallpaper
(See the directions on page 140.)

Gross Motor: Teach youngsters to do the wave! Have students sit in rows. Then prompt each row to stand, lift their arms in the air, and sit in quick succession.

Class Book: Program a page with the sentence starter shown and make a copy for each child. Have a youngster dictate to finish the sentence and draw a picture to match the words. Bind the pages together and title the book "Walter Whale."

Walter Whale wants... a waffle!

Songs and Such for the Week

Wiggle, Wiggle
(tune: "Twinkle, Twinkle, Little Star")

Wiggle, wiggle, little toes.
Wiggle, wiggle, little nose.
Wiggle arms and wiggle feet.
Wiggle wiggle—what a treat!
Wiggle, wiggle, little toes.
Wiggle, wiggle, little nose.

Wink!
(tune: "Row, Row, Row Your Boat")

Wink, wink, wink your eye—
Winking is such fun!
When you blink, you use both eyes.
This way, you use one!

W Art Activities

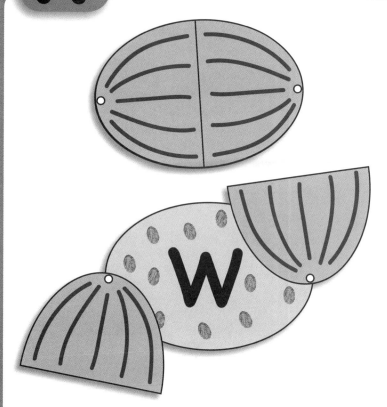

Wonderful Watermelon

To make this melon project, write a *W* on a red construction paper oval. Then press your finger in black ink (or paint) and make fingerprint seeds around the letter. Draw stripes on a green oval and then cut it in half. Use brads to attach the green halves to the red paper. Move the green halves to reveal the letter!

Patterned Wallpaper

Gather several textured items, such as corrugated cardboard, burlap, Bubble Wrap cushioning material, and fake leaves. Attach the items to a tabletop. To make wallpaper, place a large sheet of newsprint over the items and then rub the paper with unwrapped crayons. Hang the finished wallpaper in your housekeeping area.

Words

wagon	walk	wallet	walnut	walrus	wand
warm	watch	water	watermelon	wave	web
Wednesday	weed	week	welcome	whale	wig

I Can Find W!

✏️ Circle.

W

V	W	w
W	m	B	W
Y	W	w	U
W	E	f	W

Letter-sound association

I Can Read About W!

✂ Cut.

🏺 Glue the correct pictures.

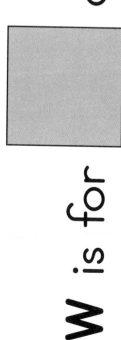

I like to say **w** words. Yes, I do!

W is for [ ] and [ ] .

W is for [ ] and [ ] and [ ] too!

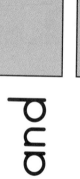
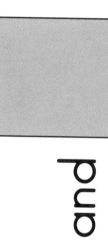

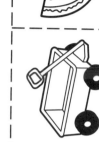

Day-by-Day Alphabet Plans • ©The Mailbox® Books • TEC61391

Centers
for the Week

 Is for...

Six: Provide a number six cutout for each child and yarn pieces. Each child glues yarn pieces to the number to make six Xs.

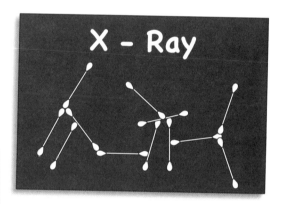

X-ray: Use a white crayon to write "X-ray" on a sheet of black construction paper for each child. A student glues cotton swab bones to the paper so it resembles an X-ray.

Box: Prepare large and small X cards (or die-cuts) and gather a large and small box. A youngster sorts the Xs into the two boxes according to size.

	Group Time	Literature
Monday	Give each child a pair of rhythm sticks (or paint stirrers or unsharpened pencils). Lead students in repeating the letter X to a simple, familiar tune, such as "Are You Sleeping?" As they sing, encourage them to tap their sticks together, making an X with the sticks each time. ***Reinforcing letters***	Cut apart a copy of the cards on page 147 and place them facedown. Gather a pair of socks and label one sock with an X. Read aloud *Fox in Socks* by Dr. Seuss. Then have a student flip a card and name the picture. If the name has the sound of X, have him put it in the sock marked with an X. If not, he places it in the other sock. Continue with the remaining cards.
Tuesday	Count the number of exit signs in your school. Write the same number of Xs on a sheet of paper and make a copy for each child. Then take youngsters on a walk around the school. Have each student circle an X on his paper each time he sees an exit sign. ***Letter recognition***	Get a pad of sticky notes. Reread the story, stopping on a page that has an X. Have a child look at the page and locate the X. Then have her write an X on a sticky note and attach it to the page. Continue with other pages.
Wednesday	Gather letter cards, including several Xs, and place the stack facedown. Have a child flip a card and identify the letter. If the letter is an X, encourage the student to lead the group in a preferred exercise. Continue until each card has been flipped. ***Letter identification***	Read aloud *Not a Box* by Antoinette Portis. Then present a box. Say, "Box," having students listen carefully for the sound of X. Then say, "This is not a box. What is it?" Have students suggest things the box could be.
Thursday	Say a word. If the word has an X in it, prompt students to cross their arms to make an X and say, "/x/, /x/, /x/!" Repeat the activity with several words. ***Beginning sounds***

/x/, /x/, /x/! | Place a box at a table and provide tape and construction paper scraps. Encourage youngsters to write Xs on the scraps and attach them to the box. |
| **Friday** | Write words that contain the letter X on index cards. Hide the cards around the room and place a box nearby. Have several children search for cards. Then have each child point to the X in the word on his card. Read the word aloud and have students repeat it, emphasizing the sound of X. Finally, have the child place his card in the box. ***Letter recognition*** | Place *Fox in Socks* and *Not a Box* at a table. Place a piece of paper in front of each book. Prompt each student to think about which book is her favorite and then write an X on the corresponding paper. |

Art and More!

Wax Drawings
(See the directions on page 146.)

Practice Page: *See page 148 for letter-recognition and sound-association practice!*

X Collage
(See the directions on page 146.)

Snack: Have each child look at a box of Kix cereal and notice the *X* in the name. Then pour each child a cup of Kix cereal to munch on!

Class Book: Program a page with the sentence starter shown and make a copy for each child. Have each youngster circle the *X* in the word *exciting* and then dictate (or write) to complete the sentence. Instruct her to draw a picture to match her text. Then bind the pages together with a cover titled "That's Exciting!"

It is e(X)citing when... my mom takes me to get ice cream.

Songs and Such for the Week

What's an X-ray?
(tune: "If You're Happy and You Know It")

Oh, an X-ray is a picture of your bones.
Oh, an X-ray is a picture of your bones.
It looks right inside your skin
To see the bones within!
An X-ray is a picture of your bones.

Extra Special!

We're extra special!
We're extra sweet—
The most excellent kids you'll ever meet!

X Marks the Spot
(tune: "Where, Oh Where Has My Little Dog Gone?")

Where, oh where has my treasure gone?
Oh where, oh where can it be?
Look at the map
Where the X marks the spot
And find the treasure for me!

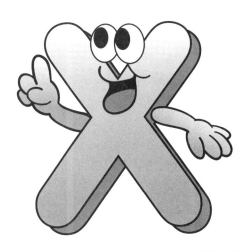

 # Art Activities

Wax Drawings

What's the key to this simple artwork? A candle! To make a wax drawing, use a white candle to draw Xs on a sheet of white construction paper. Then brush watercolors on the paper to reveal the Xs. What an excellent masterpiece!

X Collage

The result of this project is uniquely textured! Gather a variety of craft materials, such as ribbon, craft sticks, paper strips, yarn, straws, and raffia. Trim the items as desired and then glue them to a sheet of construction paper to make Xs.

 Words

ax	box	excellent	exciting	exit
fax	fox	mix	next	ox
pixie	six	taxi	wax	X-ray

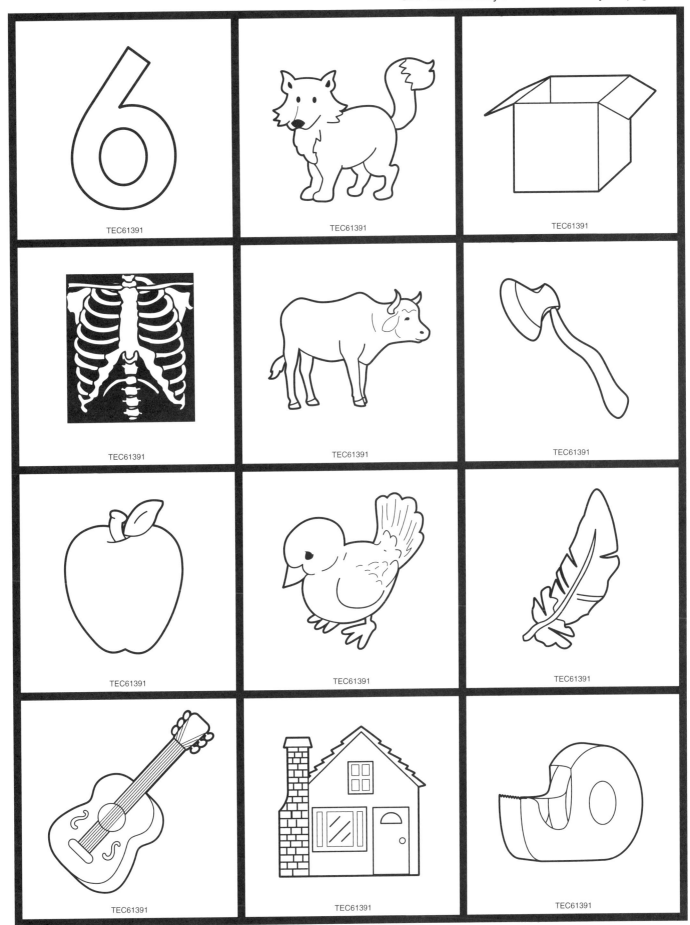

TEC61391

TEC61391

TEC61391

TEC61391

TEC61391

TEC61391

TEC61391

TEC61391

TEC61391

TEC61391

TEC61391

TEC61391

I Know About X!

Color the pictures that end like .

Circle each **Xx**.

Xx

X	t	s	x
x	K	X	c
V	X	x	X

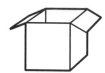

Day-by-Day Alphabet Plans • ©The Mailbox® Books • TEC61391

Centers
for the Week

Y Is for...

Yarn: Stock a center with yellow yarn cut into different lengths. Put individual letter cards for Y and y at a center. A youngster who visits the center uses the yellow yarn to make Ys in a variety of sizes. Each time she forms a Y, encourage her to say, "Yippee for me! I just made a Y with yellow yarn!"

Yolk: Label six or more yellow circle cutouts (yolks) by writing Y on four shapes and other letters on the rest. Put four egg-white cutouts, a sheet of brown paper (griddle), a spatula, and the yolks (facedown) at a center. A student uses the spatula to flip each yolk. Each time he finds a Y, he puts the yolk on an egg white and moves the egg to the griddle. When he has four eggs sizzling on the griddle, his work is done!

Yawn: To make a yawn, glue a black circle cutout to the center of a larger red circle cutout. Attach a tongue cutout and two front tooth cutouts labeled "Y." Also label an equal number of regular-size tooth cutouts for a lowercase y and an uppercase Y. A child uses the tooth cutouts to make two sets of teeth: an uppercase set for the top of the yawn and a lowercase set for the bottom of the yawn.

Group Time	Literature

Monday

Give each child a clean yogurt cup. Announce a word. If the word begins like *yogurt*, a student holds his container to his ear and says, "I hear /y/ like in *yogurt!*" If the word begins with a different sound, youngsters do nothing. ***Beginning sounds***

Give each child a yellow leaf cutout to hold. Then read aloud *The Little Yellow Leaf* by Carin Berger. Direct students to gently wave their leaves each time the words *yellow leaf* are read. Collect the cutouts to use for Tuesday's activity.

Tuesday

Get four yams. Label two yams with "Y" and two with different letters. Seat students in a circle, hand out the yams, and start some lively music. Students quickly pass the yams around the circle. When you stop the music, the two children holding the yams labeled "Y" switch places. Then restart the music. ***Letter recognition***

Reread Monday's literature selection; then redistribute the leaf cutouts. Ask students to hold the cutouts above their heads. Next, use a whispery voice to say a series of words. Ask students to slowly guide their leaves to the ground each time they hear a word that begins like *yellow*. *Shoe, cup, yummy,...*

Wednesday

Put nine letter cards that include three *Y* cards facedown in a pocket chart to form three rows of three cards each. Put the *Y* cards in a straight or diagonal line. Students take turns flipping cards. When the letter is *Y*, the group chants, "Yes, yes, it's Y!" When it is not, the group is silent and the card is flipped over. When the line of *Y* cards is found, a new game is started. ***Letter recognition***

Use a large shirt shape cut from yellow paper to introduce *In My New Yellow Shirt* by Eileen Spinelli. After reading the story aloud, ask each child to share her favorite yellow thing from the book. Then have each child use a colorful marker to write a letter *Y* on the shirt cutout.

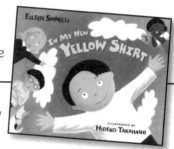

Thursday

Show students a yak and the letter *Y*. Call attention to the animal's horns and the letter's "horns." Next, stand with your feet together and arms raised to form a *Y*. Have students do the same. Together say "*Y* is for *yak!*" Then invite groups of five students to perform "Yawning Yaks" (page 151) for their seated classmates. Encourage performers to stand (and yawn) like yaks! ***Letter-sound association***

Yak

Give the book from Wednesday a fun /y/ spin! During a second oral reading, ask students to help you rename each object of the boy's imagination by changing its beginning sound to /y/ and adding *yellow* to its name. For example, *duck* becomes *yellow yuck* and *taxi* becomes *yellow yaxi!*

Friday

Ask students questions about yesterday, such as the following: Who yawned yesterday? Who wore yellow yesterday? Who ate a yellow yolk yesterday? Encourage students to name the words that begin with /y/ in each question. ***Beginning sounds***

Serve students a yellow snack and then gather the group for a rereading of one or both of this week's books. To make a tasty yellow snack, prepare individual servings of vanilla or banana pudding. Top each serving with a banana slice and a dollop of whipped cream.

Art and More!

Spectacular Yo-Yo
(See the directions on page 152.)

Gross Motor: Take students to one end of a play area. Have them stand facing you, shoulder to shoulder, in a line. Then move to the center of the area. Extend your arm forward as you tell students to pretend they are yo-yos. Explain their strings are tight and fully extended. Then use your arm and words to guide students to run toward you and away from you as you pretend to push and pull the yo-yos.

Yarn Mosaic
(See the directions on page 152.)

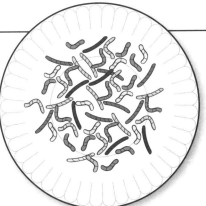

Practice Pages: *See page 153 for letter-recognition practice and page 154 for letter-sound association practice.*

Class Book: Help each child glue a paper *Y* (tree trunk) onto booklet paper. Ask what she would like to grow on her very own yum-yum tree; then have her add details to the page. Add an appropriate caption. Then bind the completed pages together with a cover titled "Our Yum-Yum Trees."

Lily's yellow yum-yum tree grows yummy strawberries.

Songs and Such for the Week

Give a Yell!
(tune: "The Farmer in the Dell")

Let's give a yell for Y.
Let's give a yell for Y.
Y is for [yes] and [you].
Let's give a yell for Y.
Yahoo!

Continue with the following: *yak, yawn, yarn, yeast, yard, yap, yolk, yacht*

Yawning Yaks

[Five] little yaks yawn a lot.
Time for bed, believe it or not!
Yawn, yawn, yawn.
It's late in the day.
So one little yak wanders away.

Repeat the rhyme four more times, decreasing the number of yaks by one each time.

Art Activities

Spectacular Yo-Yo

Working atop newsprint or something similar, fold a sheet of paper in half and then unfold it. Dip three-fourths of a two-foot yarn length in a shallow container of thinned paint. Arrange only the painted part of the yarn on one half of the paper. Repeat with clean yarn lengths and two more paint colors. Then refold the paper, place your opened palm on top of the folded paper, and pull out each yarn length. Unfold the paper to dry. Cut two same-size circles from the paper. Glue the unpainted sides of the cutouts together, sandwiching a length of yarn between them.

Yarn Mosaic

Snip, snip, snip! For scissor skill practice, have youngsters snip short lengths of yarn early in the week. To make a yarn mosaic, spread thinned white glue to cover the top surface of a small paper plate. Sprinkle colorful pieces of yarn atop the plate until a desired outcome is achieved. To secure the placement of the yarn, lay a second plate atop the artwork, press gently on the top plate, and then remove it.

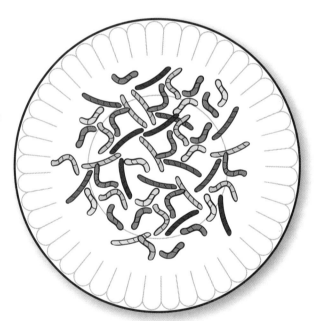

 Words

yacht	yahoo	yak	yam	yank	yard
yarn	yawn	yell	yellow	yes	yesterday
yippee	yogurt	yolk	young	yo-yo	yuck

I Can Find Y!

 Circle.

Y

y	m	Y	
y	p	Y	X
Y	S	J	y
c	Y	N	

y

Name _____

I Can Read About Y!

✂ Cut.

📦 Glue the correct pictures.

I like to say y words. Yes, I do!

Y is for  and  .

Y is for 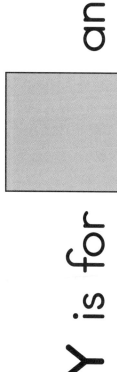 and  too!

Day-by-Day Alphabet Plans • ©The Mailbox® Books • TEC61391

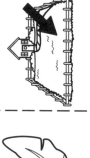

Centers for the Week

Z Is for...

Zigzag: Place masking tape on your floor in a zigzag pattern. Youngsters move toy cars along the zigzag, saying /z/ as they play.

Zebra: Attach large rubber bands to a small rolling pin. A child rolls the rolling pin in black paint and then rolls it on a sheet of white paper to make zebra stripes. Finally, she attaches a letter Z cutout to the project.

Zero: Write "zero" on a sheet of paper and provide manipulatives and a die. Two children visit the center. One student rolls the die, counts out the appropriate number of manipulatives, and places them on the paper. His partner says, "Now make it show zero." The first child counts the manipulatives and moves them off the word until there are zero.

	Group Time	Literature
Monday	Give each child a paper plate steering wheel and have her pretend to drive slowly around the classroom. Periodically hold up a *Z* card, signaling youngsters to say, "Zoom!" and drive faster. When you put down the card, youngsters resume driving slowly. ***Beginning sounds***	Read aloud *Going to the Zoo* by Tom Paxton. Then explain that the words *zany* and *zoo* begin with the same letter. Explain that *zany* means funny and clownish, and a lot of zany things happened in the book. Ask children to describe zany events from the story.
Tuesday	Label a piece of bulletin board paper "Zoo." Then hide letter *Z* cards around the room. Explain that the letter *Z*s have escaped the zoo! Then have youngsters find the *Z*s and place them on the paper. ***Reinforcing letters***	Remind youngsters of the definition of *zany*. Then reread the story, having students pantomime each animal's zany antics!
Wednesday	Name a word. If the word begins with /z/, prompt youngsters to make an American Sign Language *Z* as shown. If the word does not begin with a *Z*, students do nothing. Continue with several words. ***Beginning sounds***	Get the book *Zoo-Looking* by Mem Fox. Have students find the letter *Z* on the cover of the book. Remind students that *Z* says /z/. Then tell them that there is one animal mentioned in the book that begins with /z/. Read the story aloud. Then ask students if they discovered what animal begins with /z/.
Thursday	Provide articles of clothing, including several with zippers. Have a child write a *Z* on a sticky note, find an article of clothing with a zipper, and then attach the note to the clothing. Continue with other youngsters. ***Writing letters***	Reread the story. Then write "Zoo Animals" on a sheet of chart paper. Have students recall the zoo animals mentioned in the story. Write the animal names below the heading. Then ask students to name other animals they might find in a zoo. Add those animals to the list.
Friday	Get a zucchini and gather youngsters in a circle. Have students say, "Zucchini," prompting them to listen for /z/ in the beginning of the word. Then give a child the zucchini. Help him name a word—real or nonsense—that begins with /z/. Then have him give the zucchini to another child and continue the game. ***Beginning sounds***	Have students compare *Going to the Zoo* and *Zoo-Looking*. How are they different? How are they the same? Give each child a letter *Z* card. Have students raise their cards if *Going to the Zoo* was their favorite. Count aloud the number of cards in the air. Repeat the process with *Zoo-Looking*. Then compare the numbers.

Art and More!

Zucchini Prints
*(See the directions
on page 158.)*

Practice Pages: *See pages 159
and 160 for letter-recognition and letter-
sound association practice.*

Lovely Zinnias
*(See the directions
on page 158.)*

Z Is for Zinnia

Snack: These zebra pudding snacks are fun for
little ones to make and eat! Have youngsters help make
dark chocolate and vanilla pudding. Then have each
child place a scoop of each type of pudding in a bowl.
Encourage her to gently stir the pudding until it appears
to have zebra stripes. Then have her eat her snack.

Class Book: Prepare a paper
with the sentence starter shown.
Then make a copy for each child.
Have her identify the *Z*s on her
page. Then have her write or dictate
somewhere she would zoom to
and draw a matching picture. Bind
together youngsters' pages and a
cover titled "Zoom, Zoom!"

Zoom, Zoom!
I'm going to...
the zoo!

Songs and Such for the Week

Zebra, Zebra
(tune: Twinkle, Twinkle, Little Star")

Zebra, zebra, you have stripes.
Stripes that are both black and white.
I think you look like a horse,
Though you have those stripes of course.
Zebra, zebra, you have stripes.
Stripes that are both black and white.

Zip Your Coat
(tune: "Did You Ever See a Lassie?")

Did you ever zip a zipper,
A zipper, a zipper?
Did you ever zip a zipper
To stay nice and warm?
Those teeth hook together,
So in the cold weather,
Please, always zip your zipper
To stay nice and warm.

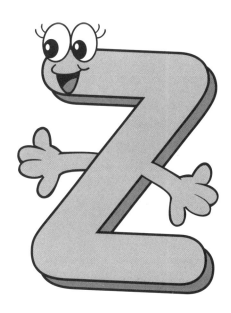

Art Activities

Zucchini Prints

Focus on the letter *Z* with this simple print process art! To make one, cut a zucchini into chunks and prepare shallow pans of paint. Lightly write a large *Z* on construction paper. Then dip a piece of zucchini into the paint and press it onto the letter. Continue with other pieces of zucchini and paint colors as desired.

Lovely Zinnias

Get plastic or real zinnias to use as inspiration. Attach a pot cutout to a sheet of construction paper and draw stems and leaves coming out of the pot. Press a bath pouf in a shallow pan of paint and then at the top of a stem. Continue in the same way with each remaining stem. When the paint is dry, write "*Z* Is for *Zinnia*" on the project.

Z Is for Zinnia

Z Words

zany	zap	zeal	zebra	zero
zest	zigzag	zinc	zinnia	zip
zipper	zoo	zoom	zucchini	

I Can Find Z!

 Circle.

Z

Z	A	z	K
C	Z	s	z
Z	X	Z	Z
Z	t	Z	Z

Name _____

160

I Can Read About Z!

✂ Cut.

🫙 Glue the correct pictures.

I like to say **z** words. Yes, I do!

Z is for  and .

Z is for and

and too!

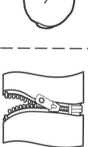
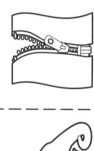
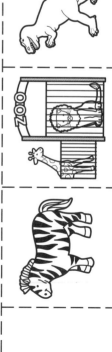